Palgrave Studies in Cyberpsychology

Series Editor
Jens Binder
Nottingham Trent University
Nottingham, UK

Palgrave Studies in Cyberpsychology aims to foster and to chart the scope of research driven by a psychological understanding of the effects of the 'new technology' that is shaping our world after the digital revolution. The series takes an inclusive approach and considers all aspects of human behaviours and experiential states in relation to digital technologies, to the Internet, and to virtual environments. As such, Cyberpsychology reaches out to several neighbouring disciplines, from Human-Computer Interaction to Media and Communication Studies. A core question underpinning the series concerns the actual psychological novelty of new technology. To what extent do we need to expand conventional theories and models to account for cyberpsychological phenomena? At which points is the ubiquitous digitisation of our everyday lives shifting the focus of research questions and research needs? Where do we see implications for our psychological functioning that are likely to outlast short-lived fashions in technology use?

Tarnveer Singh

Cybersecurity, Psychology and People Hacking

palgrave
macmillan

Tarnveer Singh
Cyber Wisdom Ltd
Birmingham, Staffordshire, UK

ISSN 2946-2754 ISSN 2946-2762 (electronic)
Palgrave Studies in Cyberpsychology
ISBN 978-3-031-85993-9 ISBN 978-3-031-85994-6 (eBook)
https://doi.org/10.1007/978-3-031-85994-6

This Palgrave Macmillan imprint is published by the registered company Springer Nature Switzerland AG.
The registered company address is: Gewerbestrasse 11, 6330 Cham, Switzerland

Foreword

In today's digital age, the very essence of our lives—our personal identities, financial transactions, social interactions, and even national security—exists in the realm of bits and bytes. The conveniences brought about by this technological evolution are unparalleled, but they come with their own set of formidable challenges. Cybersecurity stands as the vigilant guardian at the gate, protecting our digital realms from an ever-growing spectrum of threats.

This book delves into the intricate world of cybersecurity, unravelling its complexities with precision and clarity. It offers not just a technical exploration, but also an insightful journey into the human elements that underpin this field. The intertwining of technology and human ingenuity in both attack and defence scenarios is a narrative that is as fascinating as it is crucial for our time. This book explores the dual realms of cybersecurity and cyberpsychology, illuminating the complex interplay between technology and the human mind.

Cybersecurity has become the bedrock of our digital existence, safeguarding our data, systems, and networks from a multitude of threats. However, the technical aspects of cybersecurity are only part of the story. The human element—our behaviours, motivations, and cognitive biases—also plays a critical role in the efficacy of security measures. This is where the field of cyberpsychology steps in, offering invaluable insights into how we interact with technology and how these interactions can be manipulated or protected.

This book provides deeper understanding of cybersecurity and cyberpsychology. You will journey through the fundamentals of securing digital assets, while also delving into the psychological factors that influence user behaviour, decision-making, and vulnerability to cyber threats. The author is an award-winning Chief Information Security Officer and an international expert in his respective field, bringing a wealth of knowledge and real-world examples to the table, making complex concepts accessible and engaging.

In this book you will explore the multifaceted nature of cyber threats, from hacking and malware to social engineering and psychological manipulation. By understanding cybersecurity and the human psyche, you will gain a deeper appreciation of how cybercriminals exploit cognitive biases and emotional responses to breach defences. Conversely, you will also learn about strategies to enhance cyber resilience, leveraging psychological principles to foster a security-conscious culture.

Each chapter in this book is crafted to provide a deep understanding of cybersecurity principles, practical applications, and emerging trends. The author brings forth their wealth of experience, sharing not only theoretical knowledge but also real-world examples that illustrate the dynamic nature of cyber threats and the innovative strategies employed to counter them.

As you turn the pages, you will gain insights into the evolving landscape of cyber threats, from phishing schemes and malware to sophisticated state-sponsored attacks. You will also discover the proactive measures and advanced technologies that are shaping the future of cybersecurity.

This book is not only for cybersecurity professionals and psychologists but for anyone who navigates the digital world. It underscores the importance of a holistic approach to cybersecurity, one that recognises the inseparable bond between technology and the human mind. As we forge ahead in this digital age, the knowledge gained from this book will empower you to protect yourself and others, both technically and psychologically.

Welcome to the world of cybersecurity.

Cyber Wisdom Ltd
Birmigham, UK

Tarnveer Singh

Contents

About the Author

Tarnveer Singh is an award-winning Chief Information Security Officer who has worked for many decades in security and consulting roles. Tarnveer has significant experience leading information security and digital transformation. Tarnveer has been a keynote speaker at seminars and conferences discussing cyber security, technology leadership, and digital transformation. He is a Fellow of the Chartered Institute of Information Security and Fellow of the British Computer Society.

Tarnveer is a recognised author and expert on cybersecurity and emerging technologies. He offers coaching and mentoring on technology leadership. He has been recognised for his thought leadership and as a technology influencer. He is on a mission to spread greater awareness of technology and ethics.

1

Understanding Cybercrime and Criminology

As an expert in cybersecurity, I have witnessed the devastating effects of cybercrime on businesses and individuals. Cybercrime has become a major threat to businesses and individuals worldwide, with hackers and cybercriminals constantly seeking ways to exploit vulnerabilities in computer systems and networks.

Cybercrime is a criminal activity that is committed through the use of computers, networks, and the internet. Cybercriminals use various techniques to gain unauthorised access to computer systems and networks, steal sensitive information, or carry out fraudulent activities. Cybercrime is a growing concern for businesses, individuals, and governments worldwide, with the potential to cause significant financial and reputational damage.

In the modern era, the realm of warfare has transcended physical boundaries, infiltrating the digital world with a prowess that few could have anticipated. Cybercrime, once relegated to the fringes of technological discussions, now stands at the forefront of global security concerns. As our dependence on digital infrastructure grows, so too does the threat posed by those who seek to exploit its vulnerabilities.

T. Singh, *Cybersecurity, Psychology and People Hacking*, Palgrave Studies in Cyberpsychology, https://doi.org/10.1007/978-3-031-85994-6_1

Cybercrime encompasses a wide array of malicious activities, from the theft of personal information to the disruption of critical infrastructure. It is a domain where anonymity can shield the perpetrator, and where a single keystroke can trigger a cascade of consequences felt around the world. The impacts of cybercrime are not confined to virtual spaces; they reverberate through economies, societies, and even the most intimate facets of our lives.

This book explores the multifaceted impact of cybercrime, delving into its economic, social, and psychological ramifications. Through case studies, expert analyses, and first-hand accounts, we will illuminate the dark corners of the digital underworld and shed light on the far-reaching consequences of cybercriminal activities.

The economic impact of cybercrime is staggering. According to recent estimates, global losses due to cybercrime have soared into the trillions of dollars, affecting businesses, governments, and individuals alike. Financial institutions, in particular, have become prime targets, with cybercriminals employing sophisticated techniques to breach security measures and siphon off funds.

The ripple effects of these financial losses are profound. Businesses, especially small- and medium-sized enterprises (SMEs), may struggle to recover from cyberattacks, leading to closures and job losses. The cost of implementing robust cybersecurity measures further strains financial resources, creating a perpetual cycle of vulnerability and defence.

Insurance companies are also feeling the pinch, as the rise in cyber insurance claims drives up premiums and prompts re-evaluations of risk assessment models. Governments, too, are grappling with the economic fallout, investing heavily in cybersecurity initiatives to safeguard national interests.

In addition to direct financial losses, cybercrime undermines consumer trust. High-profile breaches erode confidence in digital platforms, leading to hesitancy in adopting new technologies and hampering economic growth. The delicate balance between innovation and security becomes ever more precarious in a world where cyber threats loom large.

Cybercriminals can often target sensitive data which they can hold to ransom or commercial data which could be sold to on the open market to other any other businesses or persons who would be interested in gaining a competitive advantage, for competitors for espionage purposes or for anyone who might be interested in causing reputational damage to the business.

Cybercrime can take many forms, from phishing scams and malware attacks to hacking and identity theft. One of the most common types of cybercrime is phishing, where cybercriminals send fraudulent emails or messages to individuals or businesses, tricking them into revealing sensitive information such as passwords or credit card details. Malware attacks, where malicious software is installed on a computer or network, are also a prevalent form of cybercrime, with the potential to cause significant damage to computer systems and networks. Digital DNA theft is popular through the use of deep fakes and imitation of Digital DNA. Smart and Internet of Thing (IoT) devices are easy prey for cyber criminals as the most vulnerable entry points. QR code threats are increasingly simple and commonplace. A compromised QR code can redirect you to a malicious website. Attackers like Lapsus$, exposed weaknesses with multi-factor authentication (MFA). MFA bombing, MFA bypass, and MFA fatigue became commonplace. Operational technology (OT) can also be compromised by attackers and manipulated to harm humans.

Cybercrime can occur through a wide variety of methodologies. Cybercriminals use methods like data diddling, cyber extortion, and identity theft. Often the starting point is through phishing emails or text messages which can serve as a 'can-opener' create an initial attack vector to divert people to malicious websites, to put them in touch with scammers, and otherwise misdirect them to put themselves at risk. Malware like Ransomware is something that can easily be delivered off the back of phishing emails. Malware allows cybercriminals to take control of the victim's computer, deploy keystroke loggers and then begin escalating and finding deeper routes into corporate network and/or the individual's accounts. Key logging and undermining the individual's security enables further Man-In-The-Middle attacks. Malicious actors can impersonate the individual at any moment to entice others to undermine their own security and their actions will look legitimate.

The impact of cybercrime can be devastating for both businesses and individuals. For businesses, cybercrime can result in significant financial losses, damage to reputation, and loss of customer trust. Cybercrime can also lead to regulatory fines, legal action, and damage to intellectual property. For individuals, cybercrime can result in identity theft, financial fraud, and loss of personal data. Personal information on customers can easily be sold on, financial information or health information is particularly valuable on the open market and can cause the biggest fines from regulatory bodies. Customer payment information can be used to extort money. This information can also be used to target the individual customers further and gain control of bank accounts using social engineering.

Cybersecurity means prioritising the protection of computer systems, networks, and information from unauthorised access, theft, or damage. Effective cybersecurity is essential for preventing cybercrime and protecting businesses and individuals from financial and reputational harm. Cybersecurity involves a range of measures, including firewalls, antivirus software, encryption, and employee training.

There are several strategies that businesses and individuals can use to prevent cybercrime. One of the most effective strategies is to implement strong cybersecurity measures. These may include zero-trust measures, strong passwords, and two-factor authentication to secure online accounts. Strong firewalls and antivirus also help. Regularly updating software and operating systems can also help to prevent cybercrime by quickly patching known vulnerabilities. It is also essential to be vigilant for phishing scams and to avoid clicking on suspicious links or attachments.

Data encryption is key so if a malicious actor gains access, the information cannot be used. Ensuring decent patch management is in place ensures software and apps are harder to breach. Auditing systems and removing software not being used is also important. Restricting account privileges and Role-Based Access Controls (RBAC) is important. Asking for professional advice from white-hat hackers can help businesses better understand how their security could be undermined.

Training and support through better security education and awareness is a key component. Employees should report any emails, calls or messages they see that is suspicious. Training employees so they understand security best practice, e.g., that they should avoid unsafe public Wi-Fi networks helps them avoid compromising their security. Employees should receive training to be more careful about what information they share, such as on social media which is often relied on as a treasure trove of information by attackers. Employees should question and check any requests for access, whether that is remote access by someone purporting to be in IT, or anyone else and confirm that the request is valid. Security education will help employees to better comprehend the risks and the potential impact to themselves and the wider organisation.

Technology plays a crucial role in the fight against cybercrime. Cybersecurity software, including firewalls, antivirus software, and intrusion detection systems, can help to prevent cyberattacks and protect computer systems and networks from unauthorised access. Emerging technologies like artificial intelligence and machine learning are also being used in cybersecurity to detect and respond to cyber threats more effectively.

Laws and regulations are essential for preventing and prosecuting cybercrime. Many countries have implemented laws and regulations that criminalise cybercrime and provide penalties for cybercriminals. These laws also mandate cybersecurity standards for businesses and organisations, requiring them to implement measures to protect sensitive information and prevent cyberattacks.

Investigating and prosecuting cybercrime can be challenging due to the anonymity and global nature of the internet. Law enforcement agencies and cybersecurity experts use specialised techniques and tools to track down cybercriminals and gather evidence. The prosecution of cybercriminals can also be challenging due to the complexity of cybercrime and the need for specialist knowledge and skills.

Cybercrime insurance is an essential tool for businesses and individuals to protect themselves from financial losses resulting from cybercrime. Cybercrime insurance policies typically cover costs associated with data breaches, cyber extortion, and loss of income resulting from cyberattacks.

Cybercrime is a growing threat to businesses and individuals worldwide, with the potential to cause significant financial and reputational harm. Effective cybersecurity measures, such as strong passwords, regular software updates, and employee training, are essential for preventing cybercrime. Laws and regulations play a crucial role in preventing and prosecuting cybercrime, and cybercrime insurance can provide financial protection in the event of a cyberattack. As cybersecurity experts, we must continue to work together to prevent cybercrime and protect businesses and individuals from the devastating impact of cyberattacks.

As technology continues to advance, the world is becoming more reliant on digital platforms. With this increased reliance comes increased vulnerability to cybercrime. Cybercrime is a growing concern for individuals, businesses, and governments worldwide. Cybercriminals use technology to commit crimes such as hacking, identity theft, and fraud.

In an age where technology permeates every aspect of our lives, the motivations driving cybercriminals remain a subject of fascination and urgency. These digital predators operate in the shadows of the internet, exploiting vulnerabilities for their gain. But what compels them to engage in such nefarious activities? The answers are complex and multifaceted, ranging from financial greed to ideological fervour.

Understanding the motivations behind cybercrime is not just an academic exercise; it is crucial for developing effective strategies to combat these threats. By delving into the psychological, social, and economic factors that drive individuals to commit cybercrime, we can better anticipate their moves and create more robust defences.

The most obvious and perhaps the most prevalent motivation for cybercrime is financial gain. Cybercriminals are often drawn to the promise of quick and substantial profits. Unlike traditional crimes that require physical presence and carry significant risks, cybercrime offers a low-risk, high-reward opportunity. With the right skills and tools, a cybercriminal can breach security systems and siphon off funds from the comfort of their own home.

The financial incentives are vast. Ransomware attacks, for example, can generate millions of dollars in payouts from victims desperate to regain access to their data. Similarly, stealing and selling personal information on the dark web can be highly lucrative. Credit card details, social security numbers, and login credentials are traded like commodities, with prices varying based on the quality and quantity of the stolen data.

Moreover, the rise of cryptocurrencies has further fuelled the financial motivation for cybercrime. Cryptocurrencies offer a level of anonymity and ease of transaction that traditional banking systems do not, making it harder for authorities to trace and recover stolen funds. The allure of making significant money with minimal risk continues to attract individuals to the world of cybercrime.

Criminology is the study of crime, criminal behaviour, and society's response to it. It involves analysing the causes of crime, the behaviour of criminals, and the legal and social institutions that respond to crime. Criminology can be applied to various types of crime, including cybercrime.

Cybercrime refers to criminal activities that are committed using the internet or other digital technologies. Examples of cybercrime include hacking, phishing, online harassment, and identity theft. Criminology can help explain why individuals engage in cybercrime and how to prevent it.

Cybercrime has been around since the early days of the internet. The first recorded cybercrime was committed in 1989, when a virus was introduced into the internet. Since then, cybercrime has evolved to become more sophisticated and widespread.

Criminology has been studied for centuries, with early philosophers such as Plato and Aristotle discussing the causes of crime. However, it was not until the nineteenth century that criminology became a formal academic discipline.

As cybercrime has become more prevalent, criminologists have started to apply their theories to cybercrime. Understanding the motivations behind cybercrime can help develop effective prevention and mitigation strategies.

Cybercriminals are driven by a variety of motivations. Some are motivated by financial gain, while others are motivated by a desire for power or revenge. Understanding these motivations is crucial in preventing and mitigating cybercrime.

One theory that can explain cybercriminal behaviour is rational choice theory. This theory suggests that individuals engage in criminal behaviour when they believe the benefits of the crime outweigh the risks. In the case of cybercrime, the benefits can include financial gain or a sense of power.

Another theory that can explain cybercriminal behaviour is social learning theory. This theory suggests that individuals learn criminal behaviour from others. In the case of cybercrime, individuals can learn how to commit cybercrime by interacting with other cybercriminals online.

Criminology theories can be applied to cybercrime to help understand the causes of cybercrime and develop effective prevention and mitigation strategies. One theory that has been applied to cybercrime is strain theory. Strain theory suggests that individuals engage in criminal behaviour when they experience strain or stress. In the case of cybercrime, individuals may engage in criminal behaviour due to financial strain or stress from other life events.

Another theory that can be applied to cybercrime is social control theory. Social control theory suggests that individuals engage in criminal behaviour when they feel disconnected from society. In the case of cybercrime, individuals may engage in criminal behaviour as a way to connect with others online.

Cybercrime has a significant impact on society and the economy. It can lead to financial losses for individuals and businesses, as well as damage to their reputation. Cybercrime can also have a significant impact on national security, as cybercriminals can target government agencies and critical infrastructure.

In addition to the financial impact of cybercrime, there is also a psychological impact. Victims of cybercrime may experience anxiety, stress, and a loss of trust in digital technologies.

The economic impact of cybercrime is also significant. The global cost of cybercrime is estimated to be in the trillions of dollars. This includes the cost of investigating and prosecuting cybercrime, as well as the cost of lost productivity and revenue for businesses.

Malicious actors with a variety of specialised expertise have merged to form Cybercrime as a Service (CaaS) to carry out effective cyberattacks. People and organisations are specialising in specific attack stages. There are four categories of cybercrime groups:

- Access as a Service (AaaS)—attackers who gain access to an organisation's network and sell thereon.
- Ransomware as a Service (RaaS)—attackers are extortion-based hackers. Examples include LockBit, Conti, Blackhat, Black Basta, and SolidBit.

- Bulletproof hosting—web hosting that endure abuse complaints and law enforcement takedown requests ensure that cybercrime runs efficiently and secretly. Bulletproof hosting provides sanctuaries for attackers to hoard files or malware for attack operations. Examples include Void Griffin, which was a sanctuary for APT groups and malware families.
- Crowdsourcing—this allows attackers to compare offensive strategies and attack methodologies. Competitions enables creativity especially where prizes are lucrative.

AaaS and CaaS are two examples of how cybercrime is evolving to become more sophisticated and accessible. These methods allow cybercriminals to outsource the technical aspects of their crimes, making it easier for non-technical criminals to carry out attacks. It is important for individuals and organisations to be aware of these threats and take steps to protect themselves. This can include measures such as using strong passwords, keeping software up to date, and using anti-virus software.

Access as a Service (AaaS) is a type of cybercrime where hackers provide unauthorised access to computer systems to other cybercriminals for a fee. In other words, AaaS is a way for cybercriminals to outsource the task of hacking into a computer system to someone else who has the necessary skills and software. This provides a low-risk, high-reward opportunity for both parties involved.

One of the most high-profile cases of AaaS in recent years is the Target breach that occurred in 2013. In this case, a group of hackers gained access to Target's computer systems by stealing the login credentials of an HVAC company that had access to Target's network. The hackers then sold access to Target's systems to other cybercriminals on the dark web, who used the access to steal credit card information from Target's customers.

Cybercrime as a Service (CaaS) is a type of cybercrime where cybercriminals provide tools and services to other cybercriminals for a fee. CaaS allows non-technical cybercriminals to easily access the tools and services they need to carry out cyberattacks, without having to develop the skills or software themselves.

The Mirai botnet is an example of CaaS in action. In this case, the creators of the Mirai botnet created a malware that infected internet-connected devices, such as routers and security cameras, and turned them into a 'botnet army'. They then sold access to this botnet to other cybercriminals on the dark web, who used it to carry out distributed denial of service (DDoS) attacks against various targets.

Preventing and mitigating cybercrime requires a multi-faceted approach that involves both technological solutions and criminology strategies. Technological solutions include firewalls, antivirus software, and encryption.

Criminology strategies can also be used to prevent and mitigate cybercrime. One strategy is situational crime prevention, which involves making it more difficult for individuals to engage in cybercrime. This can include implementing stronger passwords, two-factor authentication, and limiting access to sensitive information.

Another strategy is effective policing, which involves working with the community of users to prevent crime. In the case of cybercrime, this can involve educating individuals on safe online practices, cyber hygiene and encouraging them to report suspicious activity.

As technology continues to advance, the future of cybercrime and criminology is likely to change. Cybercriminals will continue to develop new tactics and techniques, and criminologists will need to adapt to keep up with these changes.

One area of focus for criminologists in the future will be the use of artificial intelligence (AI) to prevent and mitigate cybercrime. AI can be used to detect suspicious activity and respond to threats in real-time.

Another area of focus for criminologists will be the impact of cybercrime on marginalised communities. Cybercrime can disproportionately affect vulnerable populations, including the elderly and individuals with disabilities. Criminologists will need to consider the unique challenges faced by these communities when developing prevention and mitigation strategies.

Understanding the impact of criminology on cybercrime is crucial in today's digital age. Criminology can help explain the motivations behind cybercriminal behaviour and develop effective prevention and mitigation strategies. Cybercrime has a significant impact on society and the economy and preventing and mitigating cybercrime requires a multifaceted approach that involves both technological solutions and criminology strategies. As technology continues to advance, the future of cybercrime and criminology is likely to change, and criminologists will need to adapt to keep up with these changes.

With the increasing reliance on technology in our daily lives, cybercrime has become an ever-present threat that requires constant attention and proactive measures to prevent. One theory that has gained traction in recent years when it comes to understanding the motivations behind cybercrime is strain theory. We can examine the relationship between strain theory and cybercrime, the types of cybercrimes that are influenced by this theory, and prevention and intervention strategies that can be used to combat these crimes.

Cybercrime can include anything from hacking and cyberbullying to identity theft and fraud. Cybercrime has become a major concern for individuals and organisations alike, as the number of internet users worldwide continues to grow. Strain theory, on the other hand, is a criminological theory that suggests that individuals turn to crime when they experience a sense of strain or pressure. This strain can come from a variety of sources, including societal expectations, economic hardship, and personal disappointments.

Strain theory was first introduced by sociologist Robert Merton in the 1930s. Merton argued that individuals who are unable to achieve their goals through legitimate means may turn to crime as a way of coping with the strain they feel. This strain can come from a variety of sources, including economic hardship, social inequality, and personal disappointment. Strain theory has been applied to a wide range of criminal activities, including cybercrime. In the context of cybercrime, individuals may turn to criminal activities as a way of coping with the strain they feel due to their inability to achieve their goals through legitimate means.

The relationship between strain theory and cybercrime is complex and multifaceted. On the one hand, strain theory can help explain why some individuals turn to cybercrime as a way of coping with the strain they feel. For example, individuals who feel pressure to succeed in their careers may turn to cybercrime as a way of stealing confidential information from their competitors. On the other hand, cybercrime can also create strain for individuals who become victims of these crimes. For example, individuals who have their identities stolen may experience a sense of strain and anxiety as they try to recover their stolen information.

There are a variety of cybercrimes that can be influenced by strain theory. Some of the most common types of cybercrimes that fall into this category include identity theft, hacking, and cyberbullying. In the case of identity theft, individuals may turn to cybercrime as a way of coping with the strain they feel due to their financial difficulties. Hacking, on the other hand, may be motivated by a desire to access confidential information that can be used for personal gain. Cyberbullying may be motivated by a desire to gain power and control over others, or by a desire for attention.

To better understand the relationship between strain theory and cybercrime, it can be helpful to look at real-world examples of these crimes in action. One such example is the case of Albert Gonzalez, who was responsible for one of the largest credit card thefts in history. Gonzalez turned to cybercrime as a way of coping with the strain he felt due to his financial difficulties. Another example is the case of Lori Drew, who was responsible for cyberbullying a 13-year-old girl who later committed suicide. Drew's actions were motivated by a desire for attention and control.

Preventing and combating cybercrime that is influenced by strain theory requires a multi-pronged approach. One important strategy is to address the underlying sources of strain that may be motivating individuals to turn to cybercrime. This means both at a societal level and in our organisations, it is important to identify those who may be struggling most and could fall prey to cybercrime or could themselves resort to cybercrime. Support may include providing economic support to individuals who are struggling financially, as well as providing education and training opportunities that can help individuals achieve their goals through legitimate means. Additionally, law enforcement agencies can work to increase their capacity to investigate and prosecute cybercrimes, while also working to raise public awareness about the dangers of these crimes.

As technology continues to advance and become more integrated into our daily lives, cybercrime is likely to become an even greater threat. As such, it is important for criminologists, law enforcement agencies, and policymakers to continue to explore the relationship between strain theory and cybercrime, and to develop effective prevention and intervention strategies that can be used to combat these crimes. By working together, we can help to create a safer and more secure digital world for everyone.

Strain theory can be a useful tool for understanding the motivations behind cybercrime. By exploring its relationship with cybercrime, we can gain a better understanding of the types of crimes that are influenced by this, as well as prevention and intervention strategies that can be used to combat them. With continued research and collaboration, we can work together to create a safer and more secure digital world for all.

Cybercrime is a complex phenomenon that requires a comprehensive understanding of the factors that contribute to it. One of the theories used to explain cybercrime is social control theory. Social control theory is a criminological theory that explains why individuals conform to social norms and rules. According to this theory, people are naturally inclined to deviate from social norms and engage in criminal behaviour. However, social bonds and attachments prevent people from engaging in deviant behaviour. Social control theory posits that individuals who have strong social bonds, such as family, friends, and community, are less likely to engage in criminal activities.

Social control theory is based on four key concepts: attachment, commitment, involvement, and belief. Attachment refers to the emotional bonds that individuals develop with others in society, such as family and friends. Commitment refers to the investment individuals make in conventional society, such as education and career. Involvement refers to the time and energy individuals spend in conventional activities, such as sports and hobbies. Belief refers to the values and morals individuals learn from society, such as respect for authority and the law.

Cybercrime is a relatively new form of criminal activity that has emerged with the widespread use of technology. Social control theory can be applied to cybercrime by examining the role of social bonds and attachments in preventing individuals from engaging in cybercriminal activities. For example, individuals who are closely connected to their families and communities may be less likely to engage in cyberbullying because they have a sense of responsibility towards others in their social network.

Social control theory explains cybercrime by positing that individuals who lack strong social bonds and attachments are more likely to engage in cybercriminal activities. For example, individuals who are socially isolated or have weak family ties may turn to cybercrime as a way to gain attention or feel part of a community. Social control theory also suggests that individuals who lack commitment to conventional society, such as education and career, may be more likely to engage in cybercrime because they have little to lose.

Social control theory can be applied to several case studies involving cybercrime. For example, the case of the Ashley Madison hack highlights the role of social bonds in preventing cybercrime. The individuals responsible for the hack were able to breach the website's security system and steal personal information because they lacked strong social bonds and attachments. In contrast, individuals who have strong social bonds and attachments may be less likely to engage in cybercrime because they have a sense of responsibility towards others in their social network.

While social control theory provides a useful framework for understanding cybercrime, it has several limitations. One limitation is that it does not account for the role of technology in facilitating cybercrime. For example, social control theory does not explain how individuals who lack social bonds and attachments are able to use technology to commit cybercrime. Another limitation is that social control theory does not account for the role of peer pressure and group influence in cybercrime. For example, individuals may engage in cybercrime because they feel pressure from their peers or because they want to fit in with a particular group.

Future research on cybercrime and social control theory could explore the role of technology in facilitating cybercrime. For example, researchers could examine how individuals without strong social bonds and attachments use technology to commit cybercrime. Additionally, future research could investigate the role of peer pressure and group influence in cybercrime. For example, researchers could examine how social networks and online communities influence individuals to engage in cybercrime.

Social control theory provides a useful framework for understanding cybercrime. The theory suggests that individuals who lack strong social bonds and attachments are more likely to engage in cybercriminal activities. However, social control theory has limitations, such as not accounting for the role of technology and peer pressure in cybercrime. Future research could explore these limitations and further refine the theory's application to cybercrime. The implications for cybercrime prevention and intervention are that strengthening social bonds and attachments may be an effective way to prevent cybercrime. Additionally, addressing peer pressure and group influence may also be important in preventing cybercrime.

2

Case Studies: Cybercrime

Cybercriminals are individuals who use the internet and technology to commit crimes. They are a growing menace in today's society, and their activities pose a significant threat to individuals, organisations, and governments worldwide. These criminals use a variety of tactics, such as phishing scams, malware, and ransomware attacks, to gain access to sensitive information and cause damage to computer systems. We can explore some real-life case studies of individual cybercriminals and the impact of their activities.

Case Study 1: Ross Ulbricht

One of the most notorious entities to have emerged from the murky underworld of the dark web was Silk Road, the online marketplace that allowed users to buy and sell goods and services anonymously. Ross Ulbricht was the founder of the infamous Silk Road website, which was essentially an online black market that allowed users to buy and sell drugs, weapons, and other illegal goods. Ulbricht created the site in 2011 and operated it under the pseudonym 'Dread Pirate Roberts'.

T. Singh, *Cybersecurity, Psychology and People Hacking*, Palgrave Studies in Cyberpsychology, https://doi.org/10.1007/978-3-031-85994-6_2

At the helm of Silk Road, Ross led a highly sophisticated operation that used the Tor network to protect the anonymity of its users. It was estimated that the site generated over $1.2 billion in revenue before it was shut down by the FBI in 2013.[1]

Ulbricht's case is significant because it highlights the challenges associated with investigating and prosecuting cybercriminals. His activities were highly sophisticated, and he used a variety of tactics to conceal his identity and activities. However, he was eventually caught and sentenced to life in prison.

Silk Road was launched in February 2011, and quickly gained notoriety as a haven for illegal activity. Its founder, Ross Ulbricht, was a libertarian who believed in the power of technology to create a free and open society. He saw Silk Road as a way of circumventing the government's control over commerce and allowing individuals to trade freely without interference.[2]

The site was designed to be accessible only through the Tor network, which allowed users to remain anonymous and untraceable. It was a marketplace for a variety of goods and services, including drugs, counterfeit money, and even hitmen for hire. Transactions were conducted using Bitcoin, a digital currency that allowed for secure and anonymous payments.

Silk Road was a highly sophisticated operation, with a team of moderators and administrators who ensured that the site ran smoothly and securely. Ulbricht himself was in charge of the day-to-day operations and was responsible for making key decisions about the direction of the site.

One of the key features of Silk Road was its feedback system, which allowed buyers and sellers to rate each other based on their experiences. This created a reputation-based system that helped to ensure the quality of goods and services on offer. The site also had a strict code of conduct, which prohibited the sale of certain items, such as child pornography or stolen goods.

Despite its sophisticated security measures, Silk Road was eventually brought down by law enforcement agencies. In October 2013, Ross Ulbricht was arrested in a San Francisco public library, and charged with a range of crimes, including money laundering, computer hacking, and drug trafficking.

Ulbricht was eventually convicted and sentenced to life in prison without the possibility of parole. The trial was highly publicised and raised important questions about the role of the government in regulating online activity. Some saw Ulbricht as a hero who was fighting against government overreach, while others saw him as a criminal who deserved to be punished for his actions.

Silk Road had a profound impact on the dark web, and on the wider world of online marketplaces. It showed that it was possible to create a sophisticated online marketplace that was accessible only through the Tor network, and that allowed users to remain anonymous and untraceable.

However, the downfall of Silk Road also showed that law enforcement agencies were capable of infiltrating even the most sophisticated online operations, and that there were serious risks involved in engaging in illegal activity online. The case also highlighted the need for improved cybersecurity measures, both for individuals and for businesses.

The legacy of Ross Ulbricht and Silk Road is a complex one. On the one hand, Ulbricht's story has become a rallying cry for those who believe in freedom and privacy online. On the other hand, the site was responsible for a great deal of harm, both to individuals who were harmed by the sale of drugs and other illegal items, and to society as a whole.

The case has also raised important legal and ethical questions about the role of the government in regulating online activity. Some argue that the government has overstepped its boundaries in its pursuit of Ulbricht, while others believe that the government has a duty to protect society from the harm caused by illegal activity online.

The rise and fall of Silk Road highlight the importance of cybersecurity in the digital age. As more and more of our lives are conducted online, it is essential that we take steps to protect ourselves from cyber threats. Businesses also have a responsibility to protect their customers' data, and to ensure that their networks are secure from cyberattacks. Failure to do so can result in serious consequences, including financial losses, damage to reputation, and even legal action.

The story of Silk Road and Ross Ulbricht is a cautionary tale about the risks and consequences of engaging in illegal activity online. It highlights the need for improved cybersecurity measures, both for individuals and for businesses, and raises important legal and ethical questions about the role of the government in regulating online activity.

Ultimately, the legacy of Silk Road and Ross Ulbricht will continue to be debated for years to come. However, one thing is clear: the rise and fall of Silk Road has forever changed the way we think about the dark web, and the role of technology in shaping our society.

As we look to the future, it is clear that the dark web and online marketplaces will continue to evolve and adapt. While there will always be those who seek to engage in illegal activity online, there are also many legitimate uses for these technologies, from providing access to information in repressive societies, to facilitating secure and anonymous transactions for law-abiding citizens.

However, as the case of Silk Road has shown, there are serious risks involved in engaging in illegal activity online, and it is essential that we take steps to protect ourselves from cyber threats. By working together to improve cybersecurity measures, and by taking a responsible approach to the use of technology, we can ensure that the benefits of the digital age are enjoyed by all.

The rise and fall of Silk Road and Ross Ulbricht is a story that continues to captivate and intrigue us, even years after the site was shut down. It has highlighted the importance of cybersecurity in the digital age and raised important legal and ethical questions about the role of the government in regulating online activity.

As we look to the future, it is clear that the dark web and online marketplaces will continue to evolve and adapt. However, it is essential that we take a responsible approach to the use of technology, and that we work together to improve cybersecurity measures. By doing so, we can ensure that the benefits of the digital age are enjoyed by all, while minimising the risks and consequences of engaging in illegal activity online.

Case Study 2: Vladimir Levin

Vladimir Levin was a Russian hacker who gained notoriety in the early 1990s for his role in one of the largest cybercrimes in history. Levin was part of a group of hackers who stole $10 million from Citibank by exploiting a security flaw in the bank's computer systems.[3]

Levin's activities were highly sophisticated, and he used a variety of techniques to gain access to the bank's computer systems. He eventually fled to England, where he was arrested and extradited to the United States. He was sentenced to three years in prison.

Levin's case is significant because it highlights the global nature of cybercrime and the importance of international cooperation in investigating and prosecuting cybercriminals. His activities caused significant financial losses to Citibank and highlighted the need for stronger cybersecurity measures.

Vladimir Levin became infamous for his involvement in the Citibank cybercrime incident. Levin was born in 1971 in Leningrad (now St. Petersburg), Russia, and was a computer science student at the time of the incident. In 1994, Levin and a group of hackers managed to steal $10.8 million from Citibank, one of the largest banks in the world at the time. The incident shook the banking industry and raised concerns about the security of online financial transactions.

The Citibank cybercrime incident was a complex and carefully planned operation that involved several hackers, including Levin. The hackers managed to gain access to Citibank's cash transfer system, which allowed them to transfer funds from Citibank accounts to their own accounts. The hackers used a variety of methods to gain access to the system, including social engineering, network reconnaissance, and password cracking.

Once the hackers gained access to the system, they created a network of fake accounts and transferred funds from legitimate accounts to these fake accounts. They then transferred the funds to accounts in various countries, including Switzerland, Israel, and the United States. The hackers used a combination of encrypted email and telephone calls to coordinate their activities and avoid detection.

Levin played a key role in the Citibank cybercrime incident. He was responsible for cracking the passwords of Citibank employees and gaining access to the cash transfer system. Levin used a combination of social engineering and password cracking techniques to gain access to the system.

First, Levin posed as a Citibank employee and called the bank's help desk, claiming that he had forgotten his password. The help desk technician asked him a series of security questions, which Levin was able to answer correctly using information he had gathered through social engineering. With this information, Levin was able to reset his password and gain access to the Citibank system.

Once he had access to the system, Levin used password cracking software to crack the passwords of other Citibank employees. He then used these passwords to gain further access to the system and carry out the fraudulent transactions.

The Citibank cybercrime incident was a major embarrassment for the bank and the banking industry as a whole. The incident highlighted the vulnerability of online financial transactions and raised concerns about the security of the banking system. Citibank was forced to reimburse the affected customers and to invest heavily in improving its security systems.

Levin was eventually caught and extradited to the United States to face trial. He pleaded guilty to charges of conspiracy, computer fraud, and wire fraud, and was sentenced to three years in prison. The other hackers involved in the incident were also caught and faced similar charges and sentences.

Vladimir Levin's case was one of the first high-profile cybercrime cases to be prosecuted in the United States. The case set a precedent for the prosecution of cybercriminals and established the legal framework for prosecuting cybercrime cases.

Levin was charged under the Computer Fraud and Abuse Act (CFAA), which makes it illegal to gain unauthorised access to a computer system. The CFAA has since been used to prosecute many other cybercrime cases and has become a key tool in the fight against cybercrime.

The Citibank cybercrime incident and the legal action taken against Vladimir Levin have several lessons for the cybersecurity industry. First, the incident highlighted the importance of strong passwords and the need for regular password changes. Second, it showed the importance of network segmentation and access controls to limit the damage that can be caused by a cyberattack.

Third, the incident emphasised the need for strong encryption and secure communication channels to protect sensitive information. Fourth it showed the need to educate all users of the dangers of social engineering. Finally, the legal action taken against Levin set a precedent for the prosecution of cybercrime cases and established the legal framework for prosecuting cybercriminals.

The Vladimir Levin cybercrime scandal was a landmark case in the history of cybercrime. The incident highlighted the vulnerability of online financial transactions and raised concerns about the security of the banking system. The legal action taken against Levin set a precedent for the prosecution of cybercrime cases and established the legal framework for prosecuting cybercriminals.

As cybersecurity professionals, we can learn several lessons from the incident, including the importance of security education and awareness, strong passwords, network segmentation, access controls, encryption, and secure communication channels. The incident also emphasises the ongoing threat of cybercrime and the need for constant vigilance and improvement in our security systems.

Case Study 3: Kevin Mitnick

One of the most notorious individual cybercriminals is Kevin Mitnick. Mitnick was a hacker who was active in the 1980s and 1990s. He was arrested in 1995 and charged with hacking into the computer systems of several large corporations, including Sun Microsystems and Motorola. Mitnick was also accused of stealing valuable proprietary software and selling it to the highest bidder.

Mitnick's case is discussed in greater depth elsewhere in this book in the Hacker Case Studies. However, it is mentioned here because it was such an important case of cybercrime with far-reaching implications. Mitnick's hacking activities included gaining unauthorised access to computer networks, stealing sensitive information, and altering data. He used a variety of techniques, including social engineering and phishing attacks, to gain access to computer systems. He was eventually caught and sentenced to five years in prison.

However, the case was significant because it highlighted the dangers of cybercrime and the need for strong cybersecurity measures. His activities caused significant financial losses to the companies he targeted, and his actions damaged their reputations. His case also led to changes in computer security laws and regulations.

Case Study 4: Genesis Market

In 2023, Genesis Market was being run by cybercriminals with over 80 million sets of credentials and digital fingerprints up for sale. Genesis Market sold login details, IP addresses and other data that made up victims' digital fingerprints. Often costing less than $1, the personal information let fraudsters log into bank and shopping accounts.

Unlike other criminal marketplaces, Genesis Market was accessible on the open web, although obscured from law enforcement behind an invitation-only veil. Its accessibility and cheap prices greatly lowered the barrier of entry for other cybercriminals, making it a popular resource among hackers. Genesis Market operated on the open web, as well as the dark web. Set up in 2017, it was notable for its user-friendly, English-language interface. It was a one-stop shop for login data that enabled online fraud. Users could buy login information, including passwords, and other pieces of a victim's digital fingerprint, such as their browser history, cookies, autofill form data, IP address, and location. This allowed fraudsters to log in to bank, email and shopping accounts, re-direct deliveries and even change passwords without raising suspicion.[4]

Genesis Market's main criminal commodity was digital identities. This marketplace would offer for sale what the market owners referred to as 'bots' that had infected victims' devices through malware or account takeovers attacks. Upon purchase of a bot, criminals would get access to all the data harvested by it such as fingerprints, cookies, saved logins and autofill form data. This information was collected in real time—the buyers would be notified of any change of passwords, etc.[5]

The price per bot would range from as little less than $1 up to several hundreds of dollars depending on the amount and nature of the stolen data. The most expensive would contain financial information which would allow access to online banking accounts.

Criminals buying these bots were provided not only with stolen data, but also with the means of using it. Buyers were provided with a custom browser which would mimic the one of their victim. This allowed the criminals to access their victim's account without triggering any of the security measures from the platform the account was on. These security measures include recognising a different log-in location, a different browser fingerprint or a different operating system.

Login information on sale included passwords for Facebook, PayPal, Netflix, Amazon, eBay, Uber, and Airbnb accounts. Criminals buying the information were even notified by Genesis if the passwords changed.

The Genesis market had a user-friendly interface. Genesis ensured its customers had a purpose-built browser that could be used to access the stolen data to mimic the victim's computer, so it looked as if they were accessing their account using their usual device in their usual location. This was alarming as this type of malicious access did not trigger any security alerts. Malicious actors could search for potential victims by country, and see what data was available before making their purchase.

It was a very sophisticated interface, very easy to use, with a wiki (where the website can be modified or contributed to by users) telling you how to use it, and accessible on the open web and the dark web. You did not need to be a sophisticated cyber actor to get into this. You just needed to be able to use a search engine, and then you could start committing crime. Depending on how much data was available, a victim's information would sell for less than $1, or for hundreds of dollars. The most expensive data would contain financial information, such as access to online banking accounts.

While Genesis users were mostly accessing it for fraud, the data on sale could also be used for ransomware attacks where hackers block access to data and demand payment to release it. Businesses also had their information sold on the website, which facilitated fraud, mobile phone number hacking, and ransomware attacks.

The Genesis market was a monumental enabler of fraud and one of the most important marketplaces at the time for buying login information. It enabled hacking and other more significant cybercrimes to take place.

There were millions of victims worldwide. Victims would only realise something was wrong when they saw fraudulent transactions.

Genesis Market was eventually taken down. Law enforcement from seventeen countries across the globe were involved in the investigation, led by America's FBI and authorities in the Netherlands. Raids were conducted in an operation was led by the FBI in the US and the Dutch National Police, working alongside the National Crime Agency (NCA) in the UK, the Australian Federal Police, and countries across Europe. Two hundred searches were carried out and over one hundred and twenty people were arrested. The UK's NCA arrested people who were suspected users of the site on suspicion of fraud and computer misuse. At the time of writing, cases were pending against the alleged perpetrators.

These real-life cybercriminal cases highlight several important lessons for individuals and organisations. First, they demonstrate the importance of strong cybersecurity measures, such as firewalls, antivirus software, and encryption. These measures can help prevent unauthorised access to computer systems and protect sensitive information.

Second, these cases highlight the importance of employee training and awareness. Many cybercrimes are the result of human error, such as falling for a phishing scam or using weak passwords. By educating employees about the risks of cybercrime and how to protect against them, organisations can reduce their vulnerability to cyberattacks.

Finally, these cases highlight the importance of international cooperation in investigating and prosecuting cybercriminals. Cybercrime is a global phenomenon, and it requires a coordinated effort to combat it effectively.

The current state of cybercrime is alarming. The number of cyberattacks is increasing, and the tactics used by cybercriminals are becoming more sophisticated. Cybercrime is estimated to cost the global economy trillions of dollars each year, and its impact on individuals and organisations can be devastating.

Cybercrime can result in financial losses, identity theft, and damage to reputation. It can also cause physical harm, such as in the case of cyberattacks on critical infrastructure, such as power grids and hospitals.

To combat cybercrime, individuals and organisations must take proactive steps to protect against it. This includes implementing strong cybersecurity measures, educating employees about the risks of cybercrime, and working with law enforcement agencies to investigate and prosecute cybercriminals.

Cybercrime is a growing threat to individuals, organisations, and governments worldwide. Real-life cybercriminal cases highlight the dangers associated with cybercrime and the need for strong cybersecurity measures. By taking proactive steps to protect against cybercrime, we can reduce the risks associated with it and help ensure a safer and more secure digital future.

Notes

1. https://www.fbi.gov/history/artifacts/ross-william-ulbrichts-laptop
2. https://www.investopedia.com/terms/s/silk-road.asp
3. https://www.fbi.gov/news/stories/a-byte-out-of-history-10-million-hack
4. https://www.bbc.co.uk/news/uk-65180488#:~:text=Genesis%20Market%20had%2080%20million,Centre%20at%20the%20NCA%2C%20said.
5. https://www.nationalcrimeagency.gov.uk/what-we-do/cyber-crime-preventing-young-people-from-getting-involved/genesis-market-protect-advice

3

Psychology and Its Impact on Cybersecurity

Psychology focuses on the scientific understanding of human behaviour and mental processes. It seeks to explain how individuals think, feel, and behave, and how these processes interact with their physical and social environment. The study of psychology dates back to ancient civilisations such as Greece and Egypt, where philosophers sought to understand the human psyche. However, modern psychology emerged in the late nineteenth century, following the scientific method of investigation.

The origins of psychology can be traced back to ancient civilisations such as Greece and Egypt, where philosophers such as Aristotle, Socrates, and Plato sought to understand the human psyche. In the seventeenth century, Rene Descartes proposed that the mind and body were separate entities but interacted with each other. However, it was not until the late nineteenth century that psychology emerged as a distinct scientific discipline. Wilhelm Wundt, often referred to as the father of psychology, established the first psychology laboratory in Leipzig, Germany in 1879.

Psychology has since evolved into a multifaceted discipline with several branches and subfields. These include developmental psychology, social psychology, cognitive psychology, clinical psychology, and neuropsychology, among others.

T. Singh, *Cybersecurity, Psychology and People Hacking*, Palgrave Studies in Cyberpsychology, https://doi.org/10.1007/978-3-031-85994-6_3

Developmental psychology focuses on the physical, cognitive, and social development of individuals across their lifespan. Social psychology studies how individuals interact with others and how they are influenced by social norms and cultural factors. Cognitive psychology seeks to understand mental processes such as perception, memory, and attention. Clinical psychology involves the diagnosis and treatment of mental health disorders, while neuropsychology studies the relationship between the brain and behaviour.

Psychology plays a crucial role in society by helping individuals understand themselves and others, promoting mental health and well-being, and informing public policy. It provides insights into how individuals think, feel, and behave, and how these processes can be improved to enhance overall well-being.

Psychology also helps to address social issues such as poverty, inequality, and discrimination by providing a deeper understanding of their causes and consequences. It informs public policy and decision-making by highlighting the psychological factors that influence human behaviour and decision-making. For example, psychologists have contributed to the development of effective public health campaigns, environmental policies, and educational programmes.

Moustafa et al. (2021) contends in addition to computer science studies, behavioural sciences focused on user behaviour can provide key techniques to help increase cyber security and mitigate the impact of attackers' social engineering and cognitive hacking methods (i.e., spreading false information). Hence, psychological traits and individual differences among computer system users can explain vulnerabilities to cyber security attacks and crimes.[1]

As technology continues to advance rapidly, it has become an integral part of our daily lives. From smartphones and social media to virtual reality and artificial intelligence, technology has transformed the way we communicate, work, and interact with the world around us. Cyber psychology, also known as internet psychology or digital psychology, is a relatively new field that seeks to understand the impact of technology on human behaviour.

Cyber psychology explores how individuals interact with technology and how it affects their mental health and well-being. It also investigates the psychological factors that influence online behaviour, such as anonymity, disinhibition, and social influence. Cyber psychology is particularly relevant in today's digital age, where individuals spend an increasing amount of time online and are exposed to a range of online risks and opportunities.

Cyberbullying is a form of bullying that occurs online, often through social media platforms, text messages, or email. It involves the deliberate and repeated use of technology to harass, intimidate, or humiliate another person. Cyberbullying can have serious consequences for the victim, including depression, anxiety, and suicide.

Psychologists have played a critical role in understanding the psychological factors that contribute to cyberbullying. For example, research has shown that individuals who engage in cyberbullying often have low self-esteem, poor social skills, and a lack of empathy. They may also be motivated by a desire for power, status, or revenge.

There are several types of cyberbullying, including harassment, flaming, cyberstalking, and outing. Harassment involves the use of offensive or threatening language or behaviour, while flaming refers to the use of derogatory or inflammatory language to provoke a response. Cyberstalking involves the repeated and unwanted monitoring or tracking of another person's online activities, while outing involves the public disclosure of personal information without the person's consent.

Human behaviour plays a critical role in shaping the online environment. It influences how individuals interact with each other online, how they use technology, and how they respond to online risks and opportunities. For example, research has shown that individuals with high levels of self-control are less likely to engage in risky online behaviour, such as cyberbullying or sharing personal information online.

Cyberbullying has a major impact on victims. It can lead to affects (e.g., shame, sadness), mood swings (depression, anxiety and impact on long-term emotions.[2] It causes stress and psychosomatic disorder. Negative emotions in time can lead to low self-esteem, suicidal behaviour.

Human behaviour also influences the design and development of technology. User-centred design approaches recognise the importance of understanding user needs and preferences in creating effective and engaging technologies. Human factors engineering seeks to optimise the design of technology to enhance usability, safety, and efficiency.

Psychology can be used to inform the design and development of technology, as well as to promote responsible online behaviour. For example, user-centred design approaches can incorporate psychological insights into user needs and preferences to create more effective and engaging technologies.

Psychology can also be used to promote responsible online behaviour through education and awareness-raising initiatives. Programmes that teach digital literacy skills, such as critical thinking and media literacy, can help individuals navigate the online environment and avoid online risks such as cyberbullying and identity theft.

Psychology is a complex and multifaceted discipline that has contributed significantly to our understanding of human behaviour and mental processes. Cyber psychology is a relatively new field that seeks to understand the impact of technology on human behaviour, and its relationship with cyberbullying. By understanding the psychological factors that influence online behaviour, we can design more effective and engaging technologies and promote responsible online behaviour.

Cybersecurity is becoming increasingly important in today's digital world. It is not just about protecting data and keeping systems secure, but also about understanding how psychological factors can impact cybersecurity. There are numerous human factors that can contribute to the risk of cyber threats, such as lack of awareness, complacency, and negligence. Understanding the psychology behind these factors can help organisations better protect their systems from potential risks. By looking at the psychological aspects of cybersecurity, organisations can gain a deeper understanding of how humans interact with technology and how they might be vulnerable to cyber threats. This knowledge can then be used to develop better security protocols and practices that are tailored to each organisation's needs.

Taylor and Whitty (2023) contend the ever-evolving field of Information Security requires a deep understanding of human psychology. Human factors play a crucial role in the risk and threat landscape of cybersecurity, as they are the weakest link in any security system. It is encouraging that psychologists are increasingly seeing career pathways in the cybersecurity industry.[3]

Psychology plays a major role in determining how people interact with technology, and this can have significant implications for cybersecurity. By understanding the psychological factors that influence user behaviour, organisations can better protect their systems from cyber threats.

We will explore why psychology has such an impact on cybersecurity and how it can be used to improve security measures. We will look at how psychological factors influence user behaviour, as well as how organisations can use psychology to reduce risk and increase security measures.

Cybersecurity is no longer just a technical issue. It has become an issue of psychology, as humans are now the weakest link in the security chain. Understanding how human psychology impacts cybersecurity is essential for organisations to protect their data and networks from cyber threats and risks.

By understanding the psychological factors that influence people's decisions and actions when it comes to cybersecurity, organisations can better protect themselves from cyber threats. They can also develop better strategies to mitigate risk by creating a culture of security awareness among their employees, customers, and partners. Security awareness can be an effective method of driving behaviour change.[4] In addition, they can use psychological principles to create more effective security policies that take into account human behaviour and decision-making processes.

Cybercrime can be viewed through the lens of psychology. Cybercriminals, hidden behind screens and layers of anonymity, are motivated to engage in illicit activities that can have far-reaching consequences. Understanding the psychological drivers behind their actions is essential for developing effective prevention and intervention strategies. This book aims to explore the multi-faceted and complex web of psychological motivations that lead individuals down the path of cybercrime.

For many cybercriminals, the allure of the digital world lies in the thrill of the hunt. The process of breaching security systems, evading detection, and outsmarting cybersecurity measures provides a rush akin to a high-stakes game. This psychological phenomenon, often referred to as 'hacker's high', is driven by a combination of adrenaline and dopamine, creating a sense of euphoria and accomplishment.

The thrill-seeking behaviour is not limited to a desire for financial gain or notoriety. It is often rooted in a deep-seated need for validation and mastery. Cybercriminals may view their activities as a way to prove their skills and intelligence, both to themselves and to others within the cyber community. The competitive nature of hacking, where individuals strive to outdo one another, further fuels this drive.

Moreover, the anonymity provided by the internet allows these individuals to experiment and push boundaries without fear of immediate consequences. This sense of invulnerability can lead to increasingly audacious and risky behaviour, as the cybercriminal becomes more confident in their abilities to evade capture.

Meanwhile, in an era where cyber threats are ever-present and constantly evolving, the role of Chief Information Security Officers (CISOs) has become crucial in safeguarding organisations against digital adversaries. However, the immense responsibilities and pressures associated with this role can take a significant psychological toll on CISOs, impacting their mental health and overall well-being.

They are pulled into a high stakes scenario with the onus on them to maintain constant vigilance. CISOs operate in a state of perpetual vigilance, always anticipating potential cyber threats and attacks. This constant state of alertness can lead to chronic stress and anxiety. The high stakes involved—protecting sensitive data, maintaining business continuity, and ensuring compliance with regulatory requirements—add to the pressure. Any security breach can result in severe financial and reputational damage to the organisation, and CISOs often bear the brunt of the blame.

The nature of the CISO role can be isolating. While they interact with various departments within the organisation, the unique challenges and complexities of cybersecurity can make it difficult for CISOs to find peers who truly understand their struggles. This sense of isolation can contribute to feelings of loneliness and make it harder for CISOs to seek support.

Burnout and poor work-life balance are the norm for a CISO. The demanding nature of cybersecurity work often leads to long hours and an unhealthy work-life balance. The relentless pace and the need to stay updated with the latest threats and technologies can result in burnout.

CISOs may find it challenging to disconnect from work, leading to physical and mental exhaustion.

CISOs carry the weight of significant responsibility on their shoulders. They are accountable for the organisation's cybersecurity posture and must make critical decisions with limited information and resources. The fear of making the wrong decision or missing a threat can be paralysing and contribute to a sense of overwhelming responsibility.

To mitigate the psychological toll, CISOs must adopt effective coping mechanisms and seek support. Building a strong support network within and outside the organisation, engaging in stress-relief activities, and seeking professional help when needed are essential strategies for maintaining mental health. Organisations can also play a role by providing mental health resources, promoting a healthy work-life balance, and fostering a supportive work environment.

The psychological toll on CISOs is a critical issue that deserves attention. As guardians of the digital realm, CISOs must prioritise their mental well-being to remain effective in their roles and sustain their long-term careers in cybersecurity.

Cybersecurity is greatly impacted by human psychology because the success of many cyberattacks relies on manipulating human behaviour rather than exploiting technical vulnerabilities. There are many ways in which human psychology impacts cybersecurity.

Social engineering attacks involve tricking people into revealing sensitive information or performing actions that could compromise their security. These attacks rely on exploiting human psychology, such as by appealing to people's emotions, fears, or desires. For example, a hacker might send an email posing as a bank and asking the recipient to click on a link to verify their account details. If the recipient falls for the scam, they may unwittingly give away their login credentials or other sensitive information.

Phishing attacks are a type of social engineering attack that involve tricking people into clicking on a malicious link or downloading a malicious attachment. These attacks can be highly effective because they often rely on psychological tricks, such as creating a sense of urgency or using persuasive language. For example, a phishing email might claim that the recipient's account has been compromised and urge them to click on a link to change their password.

There are several types of hacking, and they can be categorised based on their purpose. The most common types of hacking are black hat hacking, white hat hacking, and grey hat hacking.

Black hat hacking is the process of hacking for malicious purposes. Black hat hackers use their skills to gain unauthorised access to data or information for personal gain. Black hat hacking is illegal and can result in significant legal consequences.

White hat hacking is the process of hacking for good purposes. White hat hackers use their skills to test the security of a system and identify vulnerabilities. White hat hacking is legal and is an important aspect of cybersecurity.

Grey hat hacking is the process of hacking for both good and bad purposes. Grey hat hackers use their skills to identify vulnerabilities in a system and may also exploit those vulnerabilities for personal gain. Grey hat hacking is a controversial topic in the cybersecurity community, and there is ongoing debate about its ethics.

Hacking can have a significant impact on the psychology of victims. Cyberattacks leave more than just digital traces; they can deeply affect the mental and emotional well-being of victims. As cybercrime becomes increasingly pervasive, the psychological impact on individuals and organisations can be profound.

Victims of cyberattacks often experience a profound sense of violation. The intrusion into their personal or professional lives can feel akin to a physical break-in, triggering feelings of vulnerability and helplessness. For individuals, the theft of personal information such as social security numbers, financial details, or private communications can lead to a loss of privacy and a pervasive fear of being watched or monitored.

The aftermath of a cyberattack can be marked by heightened anxiety and stress. Victims may constantly worry about the potential misuse of their stolen information and the long-term repercussions. The uncertainty and lack of control over their personal data can lead to chronic stress, affecting their overall mental health and well-being.

Cyberattacks can result in significant financial losses, whether through direct theft of funds, identity fraud, or the cost of mitigating the attack's impact. The financial strain can exacerbate victims' psychological distress, leading to worries about financial stability and future security.

Victims often experience emotional trauma, particularly if the cyberattack involves sensitive or embarrassing information being exposed. Feelings of shame and humiliation can arise, especially if the attack targets an individual's personal life. This emotional toll can lead to withdrawal from social interactions and a reluctance to seek help.

A cyberattack can erode trust in digital systems and platforms. Victims may become paranoid about using technology, fearing another attack or breach. This distrust can extend to personal and professional relationships, as victims question the security of communications and data shared with others.

For organisations and employees, a cyberattack can disrupt workflows, damage reputations, and strain professional relationships. The pressure to restore operations and prevent future breaches can lead to burnout and decreased job satisfaction. Employees may also face guilt or blame if the attack is perceived as a result of their actions or negligence.

Some of the repercussions of hacking can be severe. Hacking can lead to financial loss for organisations. For example, hackers can steal sensitive financial information, such as credit card numbers, and use it for fraudulent activities. It affects victims and their psychological safety.

Lives have been lost due to the psychological impact that hacking has had on victims. Hacking can also cause reputational damage to organisations. If sensitive information is stolen, it can lead to negative media coverage and a loss of trust from customers. Hacking is illegal, and individuals or organisations caught hacking face severe legal consequences, including fines and imprisonment.

To mitigate the psychological toll, victims of cyberattacks should be offered support from mental health professionals and support groups. Building resilience through education about cyber threats and adopting robust security practices can empower individuals and organisations to regain a sense of control. Organisations can also provide resources and support for employees affected by cyberattacks, fostering a culture of understanding and collaboration.

While the motivations and activities of hackers may vary widely, engaging in cybercrime can take a significant psychological toll on the individuals involved. Despite their often-stereotyped portrayal as detached and emotionless, many hackers experience a range of psychological challenges that can impact their mental health and well-being.

The constant fear of being caught is a significant source of stress for many hackers. Operating in the shadows, they must constantly evade law enforcement and cybersecurity professionals. This pervasive sense of paranoia can lead to heightened anxiety and chronic stress. The fear of detection and potential legal consequences can haunt hackers, making it difficult for them to relax or enjoy a sense of security.

Hackers often work in isolation, whether physically or emotionally. Their activities are typically secretive, limiting their ability to share their experiences or seek support from others. This isolation can lead to feelings of loneliness and contribute to a sense of alienation from society. Even those who belong to hacker communities may struggle with genuine connections, as trust is often in short supply.

Many hackers grapple with ethical and moral dilemmas related to their actions. While some may justify their activities as a means to achieve financial gain or ideological goals, others may experience guilt and remorse. The cognitive dissonance between their actions and their personal values can lead to emotional distress and internal conflict.

Despite the thrill and financial rewards that hacking can offer, some hackers may find that their activities lack true purpose and fulfilment. The transient nature of their successes and the repetitive nature of their tasks can lead to feelings of emptiness and dissatisfaction. This lack of meaningful engagement can contribute to depression and a sense of purposelessness.

For some hackers, the adrenaline rush associated with breaching security systems and evading detection becomes addictive. This addiction to risk can lead to increasingly reckless behaviour, as hackers seek out more challenging and dangerous targets. Over time, the need for constant stimulation can take a toll on their mental health, leading to burnout and emotional exhaustion.

To address the psychological toll, hackers may benefit from seeking support and engaging in healthier coping mechanisms. Building connections with trusted individuals, pursuing legal and constructive outlets for their skills, and accessing mental health resources can help mitigate the negative impacts of their activities. Additionally, ethical hacking and cybersecurity roles offer opportunities for hackers to apply their talents in more positive and fulfilling ways.

Hacking can lead to several cybersecurity threats. Malware attacks involve installing malicious software on a computer system, which can lead to data theft or system damage. Distributed Denial of Service (DDoS) attacks involve overwhelming a system or network with traffic, causing it to crash or become unavailable. Ransomware attacks involve encrypting an organisation's data and demanding a ransom in exchange for the decryption key.

There have been several major hacking incidents, including the Equifax Data Breach. In 2017, Equifax, a credit monitoring company, experienced a data breach that exposed the personal information of over 147 million people.

The WannaCry Ransomware Attack had significant impact. In 2017, the WannaCry ransomware attack infected over 200,000 computers in 150 countries, causing widespread damage.

The SolarWinds Attack was devastating in the psychological toll it took on employees spanning many organisations globally. In 2020, the SolarWinds attack involved hackers gaining access to several government agencies and large corporations, causing significant damage.

Human psychology can impact all aspects of security. Let's consider something as simple as passwords. Many people choose weak passwords or reuse the same password across multiple accounts because they are easy to remember. This makes it easier for hackers to gain access to their accounts. Similarly, people may be reluctant to use multi-factor authentication because it adds an extra step to the login process, even though it greatly improves security.

Human psychology can also play a role in insider threats, where an employee intentionally or unintentionally compromises their organisation's security. For example, an employee might accidentally download malware onto their work computer because they are not paying attention, or they might intentionally steal sensitive information because they feel undervalued or mistreated by their employer.

Psychology has a significant impact on cybersecurity because cybersecurity is not just about technology and computer systems but also about human behaviour. Cybersecurity threats can come from a wide range of sources, including hackers, phishing attacks, social engineering, and insider threats. Understanding human behaviour, motivations, and biases is crucial to identifying and mitigating these threats.

Psychological factors, such as curiosity, fear, trust, and overconfidence, can all affect people's decision-making when it comes to cybersecurity. For example, a hacker may use social engineering tactics to exploit an employee's trust or curiosity to gain access to sensitive information. Similarly, fear can lead people to click on links or download attachments without properly verifying the source, making them vulnerable to phishing attacks.

By understanding the psychology behind cybersecurity threats, security professionals can develop more effective strategies to protect against them. This may involve training employees to be more aware of the risks and to adopt safer online behaviours, as well as implementing technical solutions such as multi-factor authentication and data encryption. Overall, psychology plays a critical role in cybersecurity, and it is essential to consider human behaviour when designing and implementing security measures.

Psychology can have a significant impact on cybersecurity because many cybersecurity threats rely on human behaviour to be successful. For example, phishing attacks often use social engineering techniques to manipulate people into giving away sensitive information or clicking on malicious links.

Psychological principles such as cognitive biases, social influence, and persuasion can all be leveraged by cyberattackers to trick people into doing things that compromise their security. By understanding how these psychological principles work, cybersecurity professionals can design more effective strategies to prevent and mitigate cyberattacks.

Moreover, psychology can also help in identifying potential insider threats. Insider threats can be posed by employees, contractors, or anyone with access to sensitive data within an organisation. Understanding the psychological factors that may lead an insider to become a threat can help in identifying potential risks and mitigating them before any damage is done.

Psychology can play a critical role in improving cybersecurity by helping us to understand how people think, behave, and react to different situations, and by providing insights into the vulnerabilities and strengths of human cognition and behaviour.

Human bias can have a significant impact on cybersecurity because it can lead to errors in judgement and decision-making, which can result in security vulnerabilities and breaches.

Notes

1. Moustafa AA, Bello A and Maurushat A (2021) The Role of User Behaviour in Improving Cyber Security Management. Front. Psychol. 12:561011. doi: 10.3389/fpsyg.2021.561011
2. Kopecký, K., & Szotkowski, R. (2017). Cyberbullying, cyber aggression and their impact on the victim–The teacher. *Telematics and informatics*, Vol. 34, Iss. 2, pp.506–517.
3. Taylor, J., & Whitty, M. (2023). An Exploration of the Awareness and Attitudes of Psychology Students Regarding Their Psychological Literacy for Working in the Cybersecurity Industry. *Psychology Learning & Teaching*, *0*(0). https://doi.org/10.1177/14757257231214612
4. Chaudhary, Sunil. "Driving Behaviour Change with Cybersecurity Awareness." *Computers & Security* (2024): 103858.

4

Cognitive Bias

The assumption that individuals always have the ability to be rational and objective and thereby make decisions free from bias is defunct. We as humans are not always logical and sensible. We believe that we are always capable of analysing situations. We believe our actions are firmly grounded on the facts and correct assumptions. However, this is far from the reality. Human behaviour is often irrational. Our irrationality is especially visible during our interactions with technology. We undermine our security opening phishing emails and clicking links without thinking. This thought pattern is more inadvertent and based on instinct. This irrationality comes from bias. Lots of entrenched bias.

One way that bias can affect cybersecurity is through the hiring process. If security professionals have biases that prevent them from hiring a diverse range of candidates, they may miss out on talented individuals who could help strengthen their security posture. Additionally, biases can lead to overlooking or undervaluing certain skills or perspectives that could be important in identifying and addressing security threats.

Another way that bias can impact cybersecurity is through the design and implementation of security systems. If security professionals have biases that prevent them from considering all possible threat scenarios,

T. Singh, *Cybersecurity, Psychology and People Hacking*, Palgrave Studies in Cyberpsychology, https://doi.org/10.1007/978-3-031-85994-6_4

they may overlook certain vulnerabilities or fail to implement adequate protections. For example, if a security team assumes that all hackers are male, they may not be as vigilant in monitoring for attacks that are likely to come from female hackers.

Finally, human biases can also impact cybersecurity through social engineering attacks. Cybercriminals often use psychological tactics to trick people into revealing sensitive information or performing actions that compromise security. If people have biases that make them more susceptible to certain types of social engineering attacks, they may be more likely to fall for them.

Human biases can have a significant impact on cybersecurity, and it is important for security professionals to be aware of their biases and take steps to mitigate their effects.

Cognitive bias is a psychological phenomenon that can have a profound impact on cybersecurity.[1] It affects the way humans perceive, process, and respond to information and can lead to serious security threats. Cognitive biases can lead to incorrect assumptions, poor decision-making, and even malicious behaviour. In the context of cybersecurity, cognitive bias can create significant risks for organisations by contributing to the creation of weak security policies or inadequate threat detection systems. It also increases the likelihood of human error when it comes to identifying threats or responding to them in an appropriate manner. Understanding how cognitive bias impacts cybersecurity is critical for organisations who want to ensure their networks remain secure and protected from potential threats.

Cognitive bias must be seen through the lens of psychology as it occurs when the mind uses mental shortcuts to process information, which can lead to systematic errors in thinking. It is the tendency of humans to make decisions based on their own personal beliefs and experiences, rather than on factual information. This can lead to errors in judgement and decision-making, which can create security risks for organisations. This type of bias can have a major effect. The tendency of people to think and act in certain ways, can lead to poor judgement and decision-making. This can lead to cyber threats, as human factors are often the weakest link in security systems. Cognitive bias can be caused by a variety of factors, such as prior experience, personal beliefs, and group dynamics.

Understanding how these biases work and how they can be mitigated is an important part of any organisation's cybersecurity strategy. By recognising cognitive biases and taking steps to counteract them, organisations can reduce the risk posed by human factors in their security systems.

Cognitive bias can also lead to a lack of attention to detail when it comes to cybersecurity threats, as well as an underestimation of the risk posed by cyber threats. It can also lead to an overestimation of one's own abilities when it comes to cyber defence. By understanding how cognitive bias impacts cybersecurity, organisations can better prepare themselves against potential threats and risks.

Cognitive biases are inherent tendencies in human thinking that can cause individuals to make irrational or flawed decisions. These biases can impact cybersecurity in a number of ways.

Risk assessment is a key example. People tend to underestimate certain risks and overestimate others, depending on their personal experiences and biases. This can lead to security risks being overlooked or downplayed, and more attention being given to less important issues.

Decision-making can be heavily affected. Cognitive biases can affect how people make decisions about security measures, such as which software to use, which passwords to create, and how often to update security protocols. This can result in poor choices that leave systems vulnerable to attack.

Cybercriminals often use social engineering techniques to exploit cognitive biases in their targets. For example, they may use fear or urgency to pressure people into giving away sensitive information or use familiarity or authority to trick them into clicking on malicious links.

Biases can also affect how people perceive and respond to threats. People may become complacent or dismissive of security risks if they believe they are unlikely to be targeted, or if they feel that the risks are not significant enough to warrant action.

Cognitive biases can have a significant impact on cybersecurity, and it is important for individuals and organisations to be aware of these biases and take steps to mitigate their effects. This can include training and education programmes that help people recognise and overcome biases, as well as implementing security measures that are designed to counteract common cognitive bias.

We like to believe that we are rational beings who make decisions based on logic and reason. However, the reality is that our decisions are often influenced by cognitive biases that we are not even aware of. Social engineers and cybercriminals are well-aware of these biases and use them to their advantage to manipulate people into taking actions that may not be in their best interest. We can explore common cognitive biases and their impact on decision-making. We must consider how these biases are exploited in social engineering and cybersecurity and some strategies to mitigate them.

Restraint Bias is a cognitive bias that occurs when individuals overestimate their ability to control their impulses or actions in the future. This bias can lead to poor decision-making, especially in situations where individuals are faced with temptation or have to make choices that require self-control. Restraint Bias manifests in various ways, such as procrastination, overindulgence, and poor financial planning.

For example, a person who plans to start a new diet may indulge in a large piece of cake, thinking that they can make up for it by eating healthier for the rest of the week. However, in reality, they may find it difficult to stick to their diet and end up overindulging. Similarly, a person who plans to save money may overspend on unnecessary purchases, thinking that they can make up for it by saving more in the coming months. However, they may find it challenging to follow through on their plan and end up with a depleted bank account.

Restraint bias occurs when individuals fail to take action because they overestimate the risks associated with a particular course of action. In one case study, an organisation failed to patch a critical vulnerability in their software because they believed the patch would cause more problems than it would solve. As a result, an attacker was able to exploit the vulnerability and gain access to sensitive data.

Affect Bias, also known as emotional bias, is a cognitive bias that occurs when emotions influence decision-making, leading to irrational or suboptimal choices. This bias is especially prevalent in situations where individuals are faced with high-stress or emotionally charged situations. Affect Bias can manifest in various ways, such as overreacting to minor issues, disregarding facts, and making impulsive decisions.

For example, a person who is afraid of flying may choose to drive to a faraway destination, even though flying would be a more efficient and safer mode of transportation. Similarly, a person who is angry may lash out at a colleague or friend, even though it may harm their relationship in the long run. Affect Bias can also influence our perceptions of risk, leading us to overestimate the likelihood of negative outcomes and underestimate the benefits of positive outcomes.

Affect bias occurs when individuals make decisions based on their emotions rather than on objective facts. For example, an employee may be more likely to click on a phishing link if the email appears to be from a trusted source, such as a friend or colleague. In one case study, an attacker was able to gain access to an organisation's network by sending a phishing email that appeared to be from the CEO.

Availability bias is another cognitive bias that can lead to cybersecurity breaches. This bias occurs when individuals make decisions based on the information that is most readily available to them, rather than on all available information. For example, an organisation may focus on protecting against a particular type of attack because it has recently been in the news, while ignoring other types of attacks that may be just as likely to occur. In one case study, an organisation failed to protect against a particular type of attack because they did not believe it was a significant threat, despite evidence to the contrary.

Confirmation bias is another cognitive bias that can lead to cybersecurity breaches. This bias occurs when individuals seek out information that confirms their existing beliefs, rather than considering all available information. For example, an organisation may believe that their security measures are sufficient, despite evidence to the contrary. In one case study, an organisation suffered a data breach because they failed to consider the possibility that their security measures were not sufficient.

Overconfidence bias is another cognitive bias that can lead to cybersecurity breaches. This bias occurs when individuals believe that they are more capable or knowledgeable than they actually are. For example, an employee may believe that they can safely click on a suspicious link because they believe they can spot a phishing email. In one case study, an employee clicked on a phishing link because they believed they could easily identify phishing emails, leading to a data breach.

Hindsight bias is another cognitive bias that can lead to cybersecurity breaches. This bias occurs when individuals believe that they could have predicted an event after it has occurred, leading them to believe that they are better at predicting events than they actually are. For example, an organisation may believe that they could have prevented a data breach if they had taken certain measures, leading them to believe that they are better at preventing data breaches than they actually are. In one case study, an organisation suffered a data breach because they believed that they could have prevented it if they had taken certain measures, despite evidence to the contrary.

Groupthink bias is another cognitive bias that can lead to cybersecurity breaches. This bias occurs when individuals within a group conform to the group's beliefs or opinions, rather than expressing their own opinions. For example, an organisation may fail to consider alternative viewpoints when making decisions about cybersecurity, leading to a failure to address potential vulnerabilities. In one case study, an organisation failed to address a potential vulnerability because group members were hesitant to challenge the opinions of others.

The Illusion of Control is a cognitive bias that occurs when individuals believe that they have more control over events than they actually do. This bias can lead to overconfidence and poor decision-making, especially in situations where individuals have little or no control over the outcome. The Illusion of Control can manifest in various ways, such as gambling, superstitions, and excessive risk-taking.

For example, a person who believes that they have a lucky charm may continue to gamble, thinking that they have more control over the outcome than they actually do. Similarly, a person who overestimates their driving skills may engage in risky driving behaviour, such as speeding or tailgating, thinking that they can control the outcome. The Illusion of Control can also lead to false beliefs about the effectiveness of security measures, leading individuals to take unnecessary risks.

Cognitive biases can have significant implications in cybersecurity. Cybercriminals often use these biases to trick individuals into revealing sensitive information, downloading malware, or taking other actions that could compromise their security. For example, a phishing email that appears to be from a legitimate source may exploit Affect Bias by creating a sense of urgency or fear in the recipient, leading them to click on a malicious link or download an attachment. Similarly, a cybercriminal may exploit the Illusion of Control by creating a false sense of security, leading individuals to take unnecessary risks, such as using weak passwords or sharing sensitive information.

Mitigating Bias can be challenging, but not impossible. One of the most effective ways to mitigate these biases is to raise awareness and provide education about them. Individuals who are aware of these biases can take steps to recognise them and make more informed decisions. Another strategy is to provide clear and concise instructions and guidelines about cybersecurity best practices, such as using strong passwords, avoiding suspicious links, and updating software regularly. This can help reduce the impact of bias by providing a clear framework for decision-making.

Restraint bias, affect bias, availability bias, confirmation bias, overconfidence bias, hindsight bias, and groupthink bias can all contribute to cybersecurity breaches. As cybersecurity professionals, it is important to be aware of these biases and to take steps to mitigate their effects. This may involve implementing training programmes to educate employees about the risks associated with cognitive biases and continually improving these based on risks being encountered. We can also mitigate the effects by better understanding our employees and their likely predisposition to specific thought patterns and behaviours which make them more susceptible to potential risks, and conducting regular risk assessments to identify potential vulnerabilities and implementing security measures to address those vulnerabilities. By taking these steps, organisations can reduce the risk of cybersecurity breaches and protect their sensitive data.

Real-world examples of Bias in cybersecurity are abundant. For example, the Equifax data breach in 2017 was caused by a failure to patch a known vulnerability, which was likely due to Illusion of Control - the belief that the company had taken adequate security measures. Similarly, the WannaCry ransomware attack in 2017 exploited Affect Bias by creating a sense of urgency and fear in victims, leading them to pay the ransom to regain access to their data. Restraint Bias can also be seen in individuals who delay updating their software, thinking that they can do it later, only to become vulnerable to known vulnerabilities.

Cognitive biases can have significant implications in social engineering and cybersecurity. By understanding these biases and taking steps to mitigate them, individuals can make more informed decisions and reduce their risk of falling prey to cybercriminals. Raising awareness and education about these biases, providing clear guidelines and instructions, and staying up to date on the latest security threats can go a long way in reducing the impact of these biases. Remember, the first line of defence against cybercriminals is awareness and education. We can then start to build better cognitive models in cybersecurity and work to better predict cyberattacks and attacker behaviour.[2]

Social influence plays a major role in cybersecurity. It has been proven that people are more likely to take risks and act impulsively when influenced by their peers. This can lead to cyber threats, such as phishing attacks, malware, and other malicious activities.

Psychology also plays a huge role in cybersecurity. People's behaviour is often driven by their emotions, which can lead them to make decisions that put them at risk of cyber threats. Understanding the psychology behind human behaviour is essential for companies to protect themselves from cyber threats.

Social influence and psychology are two important factors that need to be taken into consideration when it comes to cybersecurity. Companies must understand how social influence can impact the way people behave online and must also understand the psychology behind human behaviour in order to effectively protect themselves from cyber threats.

The way we use social media and the influence it has on our behaviour can have a big impact on cybersecurity. Social psychology plays an important role in how people interact with digital technologies, and this can be used to shape the way we approach cybersecurity. Social influence is a powerful tool that can be used to increase awareness of cyber threats, encourage people to take proactive steps to protect themselves, and reduce the risk of cyberattacks. It also has the potential to help organisations better understand their users' behaviour and create more effective security policies. By understanding how social influence works, organisations can better protect themselves from cyber threats and make sure that their users are aware of the risks associated with using digital technologies.

Social influence plays an important role in the security of our digital world. It affects how we think and act when it comes to cybersecurity and can have a major impact on our behaviour, perception, and risk assessment. Social influence is a powerful tool that can be used to create a sense of urgency or fear around cybersecurity threats. It can also be used to motivate people to take action in order to protect themselves from cyberattacks. By understanding the psychology behind social influence, we can better understand why certain threats pose greater risks than others and how we can best protect ourselves from them.

Social influence can have a significant impact on cybersecurity for several reasons.

Cybersecurity breaches often occur due to human error, such as falling for phishing scams, using weak passwords, or failing to install security updates. Social influence can affect these behaviours by influencing an individual's attitudes, beliefs, and decision-making processes.

Social engineering is a tactic used by cybercriminals to manipulate individuals into divulging sensitive information or taking actions that compromise their security. Social influence can increase the effectiveness of social engineering tactics by exploiting psychological vulnerabilities such as trust, authority, and social norms.

Social influence can also affect group dynamics within organisations, leading to a culture that values convenience over security or downplays the importance of cybersecurity measures. This can create an environment that is more susceptible to cyberattacks.

Many individuals and organisations are not aware of the latest cybersecurity threats or best practices. Social influence can play a role in spreading this lack of awareness, particularly if individuals or groups with significant influence do not prioritise cybersecurity or do not take the necessary precautions to protect themselves and others.

Social influence can have a significant impact on cybersecurity by shaping attitudes and behaviours, influencing decision-making processes, and creating vulnerabilities that cybercriminals can exploit. Therefore, it is essential to educate individuals and organisations on the importance of cybersecurity and promote a culture of security awareness and best practices.

Persuasion is an important tool in the fight against cyber threats. By understanding the psychology of persuasion, companies can become better equipped to protect their data and networks from malicious attackers. Persuasion techniques can be used to increase user awareness of cybersecurity risks, as well as to encourage users to take proactive steps to avoid them. Through persuasive messages and campaigns, companies can make users more aware of potential threats and help them understand how they can protect themselves. Hereon we will explore why persuasion plays an important role in cybersecurity and how it can help us make better security decisions for ourselves and our organisations.

By understanding the power of persuasion, businesses can create effective strategies that will help reduce the risk of cyberattacks and enhance their overall cybersecurity posture. Cybersecurity is a crucial part of our lives, and it is important to understand the ways persuasion can impact the way we protect ourselves from potential threats. Persuasion can be used to influence people's behaviour and decisions, and when it comes to cybersecurity, this could mean the difference between staying safe and being exposed to risk.

Cybersecurity is an ever-evolving field that requires us to stay alert and mindful of potential threats. In order to make sure that our systems are secure, we must understand how persuasion can influence the way we perceive risk and threat. Persuasion can be powerful and can be used to influence people's decisions and actions. It has been used in marketing, politics, and even in cybersecurity. By understanding the psychology behind persuasion, we can better protect our systems from malicious actors who may try to manipulate us into making risky decisions.

Persuasion is a key factor in cybersecurity and influences how it affects our understanding of threats. We will look at the psychological aspects of persuasion, as well as its practical applications in terms of risk management. There are strategies for using persuasion effectively in order to strengthen our security measures.

Persuasion can have a significant impact on cybersecurity because it can be used by attackers to trick people into divulging sensitive information or performing actions that compromise security. This technique is known as social engineering, and it is a common tactic used by cybercriminals to gain access to networks or data.

For example, a phishing email may be designed to look like it comes from a trusted source, such as a bank or a well-known company. The email may contain a link that, when clicked, takes the user to a fake website that looks like the real thing. The user may then be asked to enter their login credentials or other sensitive information, which is then collected by the attacker.

Similarly, attackers may use persuasive techniques in phone calls or in-person interactions to convince people to give up sensitive information or to install malicious software on their devices. These techniques can be particularly effective against people who are not aware of the risks of cybersecurity or who may not be trained to recognise and respond to social engineering attacks.

Therefore, it is important for individuals and organisations to be aware of the risks of social engineering and to take steps to prevent and mitigate these types of attacks. This includes providing cybersecurity training to employees, implementing strong security protocols and policies, and using technology solutions that can detect and block social engineering attacks.

Notes

1. Darley, H. M. (2023). Dangers of succumbing to bias in cyber security: An evaluation of the impact of cognitive biases on threat assessments and cyber security strategies. *Cyber Security: A Peer-Reviewed Journal,* Vol. 6, Iss. 3, pp.211–219.
2. Veksler, V. D., Buchler, N., LaFleur, C. G., Yu, M. S., Lebiere, C., and Gonzalez, C. (2020). Cognitive models in cybersecurity: learning from expert analysts and predicting attacker behaviour. *Frontiers in Psychology,* Vol. 11, pp.10–49. doi: https://doi.org/10.3389/fpsyg.2020.01049

5

Behavioural Economics and Behavioural Science

Economics is the study of how society manages its scarce resources, and it has a significant impact on human behaviour. Entire societies and civilisations have been run on the principles of economics. Economics is an important factor in influencing behaviour on a societal and individual level. Capitalist economies run on the assumption that individuals are rational and make choices to benefit themselves. Individuals and society alter their behaviour based on economic incentives and disincentives. Other societies such as in Russia or China are based on other economic models and hence incentives and disincentives over behaviour lead to very different outcomes. This economics and the political environment may partly explain the level of state-sponsored hacking groups based in those countries.

The assumption that individuals always have the ability to be rational and objective and thereby make decisions free from bias has been proven to be far from reality when it comes to technology. We explore irrational behaviour in greater depth in other chapters. Behavioural economics studies the effects of psychological, emotional, cognitive, cultural and social factors on the decisions of individuals or collectively as organisations, such as how decisions vary from those implied by classical

T. Singh, *Cybersecurity, Psychology and People Hacking*, Palgrave Studies in Cyberpsychology, https://doi.org/10.1007/978-3-031-85994-6_5

economic theory assuming rational behaviour. Behavioural economics focuses on the limits in rationality of economic agents. We can easily be seen to be irrational at times when it comes to our own cybersecurity. We irrationally undermine the protection of computer systems and networks from theft, damage, or unauthorised access. There are often economic incentives to undermine cybersecurity. Individuals and even companies tend to focus on short-term gain. As individuals and collectively, it is easier, more efficient and seemingly profitable to skip steps designed to keep information secure. Helping people to understand the true cost, both economically and otherwise of data breaches remains a real issue. Behavioural economics governs an individual's perception of both risk and reward. An important step would be identifying social situations in which individuals demonstrate a higher tendency to discount the risk of sharing private information. For example, Individuals are more likely to reveal personal and confidential information in less-formal settings, such as casual conversation or on social media.

In today's digital age, cybersecurity is an important aspect of businesses and governments worldwide. The connection between economics and cybersecurity has become a critical area of study. The economic concepts of scarcity, demand, and supply are essential components of economics. Indeed, when one compares the modest level of earnings by Cybersecurity professionals in the West with the significant earnings by hacker groups based in rogue states, we can see how economics creates incentives and disincentives. There is a clear incentive and economic motivation for hacker groups to breach the cybersecurity of organisations, especially where information is valuable.

Behavioural economics is an interdisciplinary field that combines psychology and economics to understand how people make decisions. Behavioural economics draws on psychological factors like cognition, behaviour, emotions, and social interactions. Behavioural economics examines how people's decisions differ from what traditional economic theory predicts. Behavioural economics aims to understand why people sometimes make irrational decisions. It helps explain how people's behaviour diverges from economic models, identifying patterns in decision-making, and influencing people's decisions. Behavioural economics differs from neoclassical economics, which assumes that people make well-informed decisions based on their preferences. Behavioural economics is shaped by the work of Nobel laureate Richard Thaler, a scholar at the University of Chicago.

Behavioural economics can help us understand why Executives consistently underinvest in cybersecurity.[1] Human judgement is biased and executives can frequently get complacent and misguided that basic compliance with security frameworks is enough to keep attackers away.[2] They sometimes don't consider counterfactual thinking when the reality may be that they have just gotten lucky so far. They begin thinking there is an end point when in reality cybersecurity and risk management is an ongoing process. To counter the bias of the executives we can challenge their assumptions and use affect bias by explaining cyber risk with some emotional appeal to the high-risk areas and the likely negative impacts in financial terms for decision makers. This provides executives the complete cost of insecurity. CISOs should reframe discussion away from what has been achieved to metrics like the number of vulnerabilities to keep a constant focus on dealing with our shortcomings. This will help improve investment by improving knowledge of financial impacts and vulnerabilities. More broadly, cybersecurity economics helps us predict the behaviour and patterns of the agents and systems, design institutions, and recommend sustainable policies and regulations.[3]

If we consider a basic Security economic model we can see how we can find an optimal position between reducing potential losses and minimising security investment.[4]

Security Model:

$$V = B - C' - SI - L$$

Where V= Value, B = Benefits, C = Costs, SI = Security Investments, L = Losses

$$C' = C - SI - L \left(\text{all costs except SI \& L}\right)$$

Minimise Security Costs = SI + L

Minimise the Hacker's Gain:

$$\text{Minimise } V = B - C' - SI - L$$

We can reduce the hacker's gain by seeking to reduce their Benefit. Increase their operating costs (making stealing more difficult). Force them to invest more in their own Security Investment (making it harder for them not to get caught). Increase their losses by improving enforcement and increasing penalties and imprisonment. Our loss is the hacker's gain. Therefore criminal hacking for financial gain is worse than a zero-sum game and adds huge costs to the system. Reward good actors such as Cybersecurity professionals and ethical hackers incentivise those finding malicious code such as the Cybersecurity function and having a bug bounty programme. Punish bad actors by levying fines and disincentives on hackers and anyone in our supply chain with infected products.

Cybercrime are the criminal activities that involve the use of computers or networks. Cybercriminals use various techniques such as phishing, malware, and ransomware to steal sensitive information, disrupt computer systems, and extort money. The economics of cybercrime is an emerging field of study that seeks to understand the motivations, incentives, and economic consequences of cybercriminal activities.

One of the key economic drivers of cybercrime is the potential for financial gain. Information is a highly valuable economic resource in itself. Corporations and Nation states are willing to pay millions of dollars for access to sensitive information. Information can be sold on anonymously on the dark web through cryptocurrency so there is no easy audit trail, and the risk is pretty low, especially if you reside in a country that does not have an extradition treaty for cybercrime. The fines by regulators for data breaches by corporations and organisations can reach into millions of dollars as well. So, cybercrime can be both economically lucrative and be seen as a weapon against adversaries. Cybersecurity professionals earn a fraction of what hacking groups can earn.

Cybercriminals are motivated by the possibility of making money through various means such as stealing credit card details, conducting ransomware attacks, or selling stolen data on the dark web. The economic gains from cybercrime can be significant, making it an attractive option for criminals.

Another economic driver of cybercrime is the low risk of being caught and punished. Cybercriminals can operate from anywhere in the world and often use sophisticated techniques to hide their tracks. The low risk of being caught and punished makes cybercrime an attractive option for criminals, as they can make significant profits without fear of repercussions.

Case Study 1: The WannaCry Ransomware Attack

One of the most significant cyberattacks in recent times was the WannaCry ransomware attack that occurred in May 2017. The attack affected over 200,000 computers in 150 countries and caused billions of dollars in damages. The WannaCry ransomware encrypted users' files and demanded payment in bitcoin to regain access to their data.[5]

The economic consequences of the WannaCry attack were significant. Many businesses and organisations had to shut down their operations temporarily, leading to lost revenue and productivity. The attack also highlighted the vulnerabilities in many computer systems and the need for better cybersecurity measures.

Case Study 2: The Equifax Data Breach

The Equifax data breach is another example of the economic consequences of cybercrime. Equifax, one of the largest credit bureaus in the United States, suffered a major data breach. The economic impact of this breach was significant, with Equifax estimating that the cost of the breach could reach $600 million. The breach, which occurred in 2017, exposed the personal information of over 147 million people. The information included names, addresses, birth dates, and social security numbers, making it a significant breach of sensitive data.[6]

The economic impact of the Equifax breach was significant. Many people had to cancel their credit cards and monitor their credit reports for fraudulent activity, leading to lost time and money. The breach also led to a loss of trust in Equifax and the credit reporting industry as a whole.

The breach had a direct impact on the company's stock price, which dropped by nearly 14% in the days following the incident. Furthermore, Equifax had to spend millions of dollars on legal fees, cybersecurity improvements, and compensation for affected customers. The long-term impact of the breach on the company's reputation and customer trust remains to be seen.

Case Study 3: NotPetya

NotPetya is a ransomware attack that occurred in 2017, targeting businesses and governments worldwide. The attack spread through a software update and encrypted users' files, demanding payment in bitcoin to regain access. The economic consequences of NotPetya were significant, with estimates of damages ranging from $4 billion to $10 billion.[7]

The NotPetya attack highlighted the need for better cybersecurity measures and the economic impact of cybercrime. The attack affected businesses and governments worldwide and led to lost productivity and revenue.

Case Study 4: The Sony Pictures Hack

In 2014, Sony Pictures Entertainment was the victim of a cyberattack that resulted in the theft of sensitive data, including employee personal information, unreleased films, and confidential emails. The hackers responsible for the attack were allegedly linked to North Korea, and the incident was believed to be in retaliation for the release of the movie "The Interview."

The economic impact of the Sony Pictures hack was significant, with the company estimating that the cost of the breach could reach $100 million. The company had to deal with a wide range of issues, including lost revenue from cancelled movie releases, reputational damage, and legal fees.[8]

Case Study 5: The Target Data Breach

In 2013, Target Corporation suffered a data breach that resulted in the theft of millions of customers' credit and debit card information. The breach had a significant economic impact on the company, with Target estimating that the cost of the breach was $252 million.[9]

The impact of the breach on the company's reputation was also significant, with a decline in customer trust and loyalty. The company had to spend millions of dollars to improve its cybersecurity measures and provide compensation to affected customers.

Case Study 6: The Bangladesh Bank Heist

In 2016, hackers successfully stole $81 million from the Bangladesh Bank's account at the Federal Reserve Bank of New York. The hackers used fraudulent SWIFT messages to transfer the money to accounts in the Philippines and Sri Lanka.[10]

The economic impact of the Bangladesh Bank heist was significant. The stolen funds represented a significant portion of the country's foreign exchange reserves, and the incident raised concerns about the security of the global financial system.

Case Study 7: The Yahoo Data Breach

In 2016, it was revealed that Yahoo had suffered a massive data breach in 2013 that resulted in the theft of personal information from all three billion of its user accounts. The economic impact of the breach was significant, with the company estimating that the cost of the breach was $350 million.[11]

The breach had a significant impact on the company's reputation and customer trust. The incident also raised concerns about the security of other major technology companies and the safety of personal information on the internet.

The economic impact of hacking incidents can be significant, with costs ranging from millions to billions of dollars. Companies must take proactive steps to prevent cyberattacks and protect their sensitive data and the data of their customers.

As individuals, it is also essential to take measures to protect our personal information, such as using strong passwords, avoiding suspicious emails and links, and regularly updating our software and security measures.

By understanding the economic impacts of hacking, we can all take steps to protect ourselves and our businesses from the devastating effects of cyberattacks.

The economic consequences of cybercrime affect businesses, governments, and individuals worldwide. Cybercrime can lead to lost revenue, lost productivity, and increased costs associated with cybersecurity measures. The economic impact of cybercrime can also lead to a loss of trust in businesses and governments, affecting their reputation and long-term viability.

The costs of cybercrime can be difficult to quantify, as they may include both direct and indirect costs. Direct costs may include the costs associated with cybersecurity measures, such as software and hardware upgrades, while indirect costs may include lost productivity and lost revenue.

Economics can create disincentives for cybercrime by increasing the cost of engaging in criminal activities. One way to achieve this is by increasing the risk of being caught and punished. Governments can increase the penalties for cybercrime, making it a less attractive option for criminals.

Another way to create disincentives for cybercrime is by increasing the cost of engaging in criminal activities. Governments can invest in cybersecurity measures, making it harder for criminals to carry out cyberattacks. This can include measures such as better encryption, increased training for employees, and better monitoring of computer systems.

Preventing cybercrime requires a comprehensive approach that involves both technological and economic measures. Technological measures can include better encryption, more robust firewalls, and improved monitoring of computer systems. Economic measures can include increasing the risk and cost of engaging in cybercrime, as well as investing in cybersecurity measures.

Governments, businesses, and individuals all have a role to play in preventing cybercrime. Governments can invest in cybersecurity measures and increase the penalties for cybercrime. Businesses can invest in better cybersecurity measures and train their employees to recognise and prevent cyberattacks. Individuals can take steps to protect their personal information, such as using strong passwords and avoiding suspicious emails. Security professionals are working closer with governmental bodies and as a result are increasingly changing their approach to find ways to not pay ransomware and other cybercrime. This challenges the economics of hacking and cyberattacks.

As technology continues to advance, the intersection of economics and cybersecurity will become increasingly important. The economic consequences of cybercrime will continue to be significant, affecting businesses, governments, and individuals worldwide. The role of economics in preventing and deterring cybercrime will become increasingly important, as governments and businesses seek to protect themselves and their customers from cyberattacks.

The economics of cybercrime is an emerging field of study that seeks to understand the motivations, incentives, and economic consequences of cybercriminal activities. The economic consequences of cybercrime can be significant, affecting businesses, governments, and individuals worldwide. Preventing cybercrime requires a comprehensive approach that involves both technological and economic measures. As technology continues to advance, the role of economics in cybersecurity will become increasingly important. Governments, businesses, and individuals all have a role to play in preventing cybercrime and protecting themselves from cyberattacks.

Behavioural science is a multidisciplinary field that explores the nuances of human behaviour. It involves the study of social and cognitive processes, emotions and motivations, decision-making, and the factors that influence human behaviour. Behavioural science draws on a range of disciplines, including psychology, sociology, anthropology, economics, and neuroscience. If we truly desire to improve cybersecurity we must delve into behavioural science, its key concepts, applications, and the role it plays in cyber. Behavioural science theories are vital in understanding the influence of human factors in cybersecurity.[12] We should explore the ethical considerations in behavioural science research, behavioural science and cybercrime, and the future of behavioural science.

Behavioural science has its roots in psychology. The early pioneers of psychology, such as Wilhelm Wundt, William James, and Sigmund Freud, paved the way for the development of behavioural science. However, it wasn't until the mid-twentieth century that behavioural science took shape as a distinct field of study.

In the 1950s, psychologists such as B.F. Skinner and Albert Bandura began to focus on the role of external stimuli in shaping behaviour. They believed that behaviour was a product of environmental factors, and that by manipulating those factors, they could influence behaviour. This led to the development of behaviourism, which became a dominant force in psychology for several decades.

Behaviourism was later challenged by cognitive psychology, which focused on the internal processes that underlie behaviour, such as attention, perception, memory, and reasoning. Cognitive psychology paved the way for the development of cognitive-behavioural therapy, which is now a widely used treatment for mental health problems.

Behavioural science encompasses a range of key concepts that are central to understanding human behaviour. These include motivation, emotion, learning, perception, and decision-making. Motivation is the driving force behind behaviour, and it can be either intrinsic or extrinsic. Emotions play a crucial role in decision-making, and they can influence behaviour in profound ways. Learning is the process by which behaviour is acquired, and it can occur through classical conditioning, operant conditioning, or observation. Perception is the interpretation of sensory information, and it plays a critical role in shaping behaviour.

Psychology is a subdiscipline of behavioural science, which is an interdisciplinary field that studies human behaviour. Psychology focuses on the mental processes that underlie behaviour, while behavioural science takes a broader perspective and emphasises behavioural outcomes.

Behavioural science combines insights from psychology with other disciplines, such as sociology, neuroscience, economics, and political science. Behavioural scientists use their knowledge to develop interventions to change behaviour or to design policies that encourage people to act in a certain way. These insights are often applied to areas like public policy, healthcare, and marketing.

Behavioural scientists use a variety of research methods, including experimentation, observation, genetics, neuroimaging, and self-report studies.

Behavioural scientists synthesise theories and concepts from different disciplines to understand human behaviour. For example, behavioural economics is a field that applies psychological insights to economic behaviour.

Decision-making is a complex process that involves multiple factors, including emotions, cognition, and social influences. Behavioural science has identified biases that can affect decision-making, such as confirmation bias, availability bias, and anchoring bias. By understanding these biases, researchers can develop interventions to improve decision-making in various contexts.

Behavioural science has a wide range of applications in various fields, including healthcare, finance, marketing, and public policy. In healthcare, behavioural science is used to promote healthy behaviours, such as exercise and healthy eating. It is also used to develop interventions to improve patient adherence to medication regimens.

In finance, behavioural science is used to understand investor behaviour and to develop strategies to promote better investment decisions. In marketing, behavioural science is used to develop more effective advertising campaigns and to improve customer engagement. In public policy, behavioural science is used to develop interventions to promote civic engagement and to improve public health outcomes.

As a cybersecurity expert, I have come to realise that the most significant threat to cybersecurity is not the technology itself, but human behaviour. That's where behavioural science comes in. Behavioural science is the study of human behaviour, and it is increasingly becoming essential in cybersecurity. We can consider the role of behavioural science in cybersecurity, the psychology of cybercrime, and the impact of social engineering on cybersecurity. We can also explore behavioural science-based cybersecurity solutions, case studies on the application of behavioural science in cybersecurity, challenges in implementing behavioural science in cybersecurity, future trends in behavioural science and cybersecurity, and the importance of behavioural science in cybersecurity training.

Behavioural science plays an important role in cybersecurity. Cyberattackers often use social engineering techniques to trick people into revealing sensitive information or to gain access to computer systems. Behavioural science can be used to understand these techniques and to develop interventions to prevent them.

For example, phishing attacks are a common type of social engineering attack. By understanding the psychological principles that underlie phishing attacks, such as authority, urgency, and social proof, cybersecurity professionals can design interventions to prevent them. These interventions may include training employees to recognise phishing attacks, implementing two-factor authentication, and using behavioural analysis tools to detect suspicious activity.

Behavioural science is already helping improve cybersecurity. For example the science has helped identify that personality traits, such as impulsivity, risk taking, and lack of thinking about future consequences of actions, are related to a lack of compliance with cyber and network security policies.[13] Psychological methods can increase pro-security behaviours, such as rewarding and penalising security-related behaviours, using novel polymorphic security warnings, and using psychological methods to increase thinking about future consequences of actions.

Behavioural science also has a significant impact on technology. The design of technology products and services can be influenced by behavioural science principles. For example, social media platforms use behavioural science to design features that keep users engaged, such as notifications and likes. E-commerce websites use behavioural science to design product recommendations and pricing strategies that increase sales.

However, the impact of behavioural science on technology is not always positive. Technology can also have negative impacts on behaviour, such as addiction, distraction, and social isolation. Behavioural science can be used to design interventions to address these negative impacts, such as digital detox programmes and mindfulness apps.

Behavioural science research raises several ethical considerations. One of the most significant issues is informed consent. Participants in behavioural science research must be fully informed about the purpose of the study, the risks and benefits, and their right to withdraw at any time. Researchers must also ensure that participants are not coerced into participating and that their privacy is protected.

Another ethical consideration is the use of deception in research. Deception can be used to study sensitive topics or to avoid bias, but it must be justified by the potential benefits of the research. Researchers must also ensure that participants are debriefed after the study and that any negative effects are addressed.

Behavioural science is also used to study cybercrime. Cybercriminals use a range of techniques to deceive and manipulate their victims, and behavioural science can be used to understand these techniques and to develop interventions to prevent them.

For example, cybercriminals often use social engineering techniques to trick people into revealing sensitive information or to gain access to computer systems. By understanding the psychological principles that underlie these techniques, cybersecurity professionals can design interventions to prevent them.

Human behaviour is unpredictable, and this makes it difficult to predict cybersecurity risks. However, by understanding human behaviour, we can identify potential risks and take the necessary measures to mitigate them. For instance, we know that people tend to use simple passwords that are easy to remember. This behaviour puts them at risk of cyberattacks because hackers can easily guess their passwords. By understanding this behaviour, we can create policies that require people to use strong passwords.

Communication with the cybersecurity function can reduce risk created by human factors.[14] Encouraging communication of concerns and risks allows for procedures and plans to be improved. Complacency leads to false confidence by employees. Employees can feel that because poor cyber practices have been allowed to fester but have not yet led to a breach then they are safe. This complacency must be constantly challenged. Distraction is often a tactic used by cybercriminals. Hackers try to understand how IT teams work, and they research ways of working in the organisations they target so they can better exploit the dysfunction. Fatigue is often a causal factor. A stressful working environment can cause pressure and undermine cyber hygiene. If assertiveness by employees is poor this can reduce the reporting of risks. We must encourage anonymous reporting of risks. Lack of awareness reduces vigilance. Norms of behaviour in workplace practices can themselves lead to unsafe behaviour, and exploitation by cyber criminals. Hence it is important to conduct regular tests to see how well employees understand their responsibilities in incident response plans, disaster recovery or business continuity plans.

We know that people tend to click on links without verifying their authenticity. This behaviour puts them at risk of phishing attacks. By understanding this behaviour, we can educate people on how to identify phishing attacks and avoid them. Understanding human behaviour is, therefore, critical in identifying potential cybersecurity risks and developing effective cybersecurity strategies.

Cybercriminals use various psychological tactics to lure their victims into falling for their tricks. For instance, they may use fear, urgency, or curiosity to get people to click on links or download attachments. They may also use social engineering tactics, such as pretexting or baiting, to gain access to sensitive information. By understanding the psychology of cybercrime, we can develop effective strategies to protect ourselves from cyberattacks.

One of the most common psychological tactics used by cybercriminals is social proof. Social proof is the tendency to follow the actions of others. Cybercriminals use social proof to create a sense of urgency or fear, making people act without thinking. For instance, a cybercriminal may send an email claiming that a person's account has been hacked and that they need to change their password immediately. The email may include a link to a fake login page that captures the person's login details. By understanding this psychology, we can educate people on how to identify and avoid social engineering attacks.

Social engineering is a technique used by cybercriminals to manipulate people into giving up sensitive information. Social engineering attacks are prevalent because they exploit human weaknesses. Social engineering attacks can take various forms, such as phishing, pretexting, baiting, or quid pro quo. By understanding the impact of social engineering on cybersecurity, we can develop effective strategies to prevent these attacks.

One of the most common social engineering attacks is phishing. Phishing attacks use emails or text messages to trick people into providing sensitive information, such as login credentials or credit card details. These attacks can be challenging to detect because they often appear to come from legitimate sources. By educating people on how to identify phishing attacks, we can prevent them from falling for these scams.

Behavioural science can be used to develop effective cybersecurity solutions. For instance, we can use behavioural science to design user interfaces that encourage people to follow security policies. We can also use behavioural science to develop training programmes that teach people how to identify and avoid social engineering attacks. Behavioural science can also be used to develop incentives that encourage people to follow security policies.

Galvão et al. (2023) argue for the increasing use of AI in cybersecurity through effective AI development understanding behavioural psychology and how users interact with and respond so that more effective and aware cybersecurity systems can be created and implemented.[15]

Another effective behavioural science-based cybersecurity solutions is two-factor authentication. Two-factor authentication requires people to provide two forms of identification before accessing sensitive information. This solution is effective because it makes it difficult for cybercriminals to gain access to sensitive information even if they have the login credentials. By using behavioural science-based cybersecurity solutions, we can reduce the likelihood of cyberattacks.

Rich et al. (2024) argue that cyber behavioural sciences and digital forensics can help to improve the prediction and effectiveness of cyber threats by combining technical expertise with cybercriminal behaviour insights to enable more accurate prediction of cyber threats.[16]

One of the biggest challenges in implementing behavioural science in cybersecurity is resistance to change. People are often resistant to change and implementing new policies or procedures can be challenging. Another challenge is the lack of expertise in behavioural science among cybersecurity professionals. Behavioural science is a relatively new field, and there are few experts in this area. This makes it difficult to develop effective behavioural science-based cybersecurity solutions.

Behavioural science is essential in cybersecurity training. By understanding human behaviour, we can develop effective training programmes that teach people how to identify and avoid potential cybersecurity risks. Behavioural science can also be used to develop incentives that encourage people to follow security policies. By incorporating behavioural science into cybersecurity training, we can reduce the likelihood of cyberattacks.

As technology continues to evolve, the need for a deeper understanding of human behaviour will only increase. Behavioural science will play an important role in designing technology products and services that promote positive behaviours and prevent negative behaviours.

Behavioural science will also continue to be an important tool in addressing societal challenges, such as public health, climate change, and social inequality. As the field of behavioural science continues to evolve, researchers will develop new theories and methodologies to better understand human behaviour and to develop more effective interventions.

Behavioural science is a fascinating and rapidly evolving field that has applications in a wide range of domains. Its key concepts, such as motivation, emotion, learning, perception, and decision-making, provide valuable insights into human behaviour. Behavioural science has important implications for cybersecurity, technology, and public policy. As the field continues to evolve, it will play an increasingly important role in addressing societal challenges and improving human well-being.

Warrington et al. (2022) argue that employee personality traits can have a significant impact on information security behaviour. They argue that personality traits like extraversion, agreeableness, conscientiousness, emotional stability, and intellect can all impact on security.[17]

Behavioural science will continue to play an increasing role in cybersecurity. As technology continues to evolve, cybercriminals will develop new tactics, and behavioural science will be critical in developing effective cybersecurity strategies. One of the future trends in behavioural science and cybersecurity is the use of artificial intelligence. Artificial intelligence can be used to identify potential cybersecurity risks and develop effective cybersecurity solutions.

By understanding human behaviour, we can identify potential cybersecurity risks and develop effective cybersecurity strategies. The psychology of cybercrime and the impact of social engineering on cybersecurity highlight the importance of behavioural science in developing effective cybersecurity solutions. Behavioural science-based cybersecurity solutions, case studies on the application of behavioural science in cybersecurity, challenges in implementing behavioural science in cybersecurity, future trends in behavioural science and cybersecurity, and the importance of behavioural science in cybersecurity training demonstrate the many ways in which behavioural science can be used to enhance cybersecurity.

Notes

1. https://hbr.org/2017/06/the-behavioral-economics-of-why-executives-underinvest-in-cybersecurity
2. Fineberg, V. (2014). BEC: Applying behavioral economics to harden cyberspace. *J Cyber Secur Inf Syst*, Vol. 2, Iss. 1, pp.27–33.
3. Kianpour, M., Kowalski, S. J., & Øverby, H. (2021). Systematically understanding cybersecurity economics: A survey. *Sustainability*, Vol. 13, Iss. 24, 13677.
4. Beckstrom, R. (2009). Economics Of Networks - Rod Beckstrom, National Cybersecurity Center, Department of Homeland Security
5. https://www.kaspersky.com/resource-center/threats/ransomware-wannacry
6. https://www.csoonline.com/article/567833/equifax-data-breach-faq-what-happened-who-was-affected-what-was-the-impact.html
7. https://www.wired.com/story/notpetya-cyberattack-ukraine-russia-code-crashed-the-world/
8. https://coverlink.com/case-study/sony-pictures-entertainment-hack/
9. https://www.reuters.com/article/us-target-cyber-settlement/target-in-18-5-million-multi-state-settlement-over-data-breach-idUSKBN18J2GH/

10. https://www.wired.com/2016/05/insane-81m-bangladesh-bank-heist-heres-know/
11. https://www.nytimes.com/2017/10/03/technology/yahoo-hack-3-billion-users.html
12. Kadena, E., & Gupi, M. (2021). Human Factors in Cybersecurity: Risks and Impacts. *Security Science Journal*, Vol. 2, Iss. 2, pp.51–64.
13. Moustafa, A.A., Bello, A., and Maurushat, A. (2021). The Role of User Behaviour in Improving Cyber Security Management. *Frontiers in Psychology*, Vol. 12 No. 2, pp. 72–77. https://doi.org/10.3389/fpsyg.2021.561011
14. Kadena, E., & Gupi, M. (2021). Human Factors in Cybersecurity: Risks and Impacts. *Security Science Journal*, Vol. 2, Iss. 2, pp. 51–64.
15. Galvão, A., Chumbo, I., & Anes, E. (2023). Behavioural Psychology Towards Artificial Intelligence in Cybersecurity. In N. Mateus-Coelho & M. Cruz-Cunha (Eds.), *Exploring Cyber Criminals and Data Privacy Measures* (pp. 19–39). IGI Global. https://doi.org/10.4018/978-1-6684-8422-7.ch002
16. Rich, Marshall S., and Mary P. Aiken. "An Interdisciplinary Approach to Enhancing Cyber Threat Prediction Utilizing Forensic Cyberpsychology and Digital Forensics." *Forensic Sciences* 4.1 (2024): 110–151.
17. Warrington, C., Syed, J., & Tappin, R. M. (2022). Personality and Employees' Information Security Behavior Among Generational Cohorts. *Journal of Organizational Psychology, 22*(3). Retrieved from https://articlearchives.co/index.php/JOP/article/view/5287

6

Neuroscience, Sociology, and Anthropology

Psychology and neuroscience are closely related fields that complement each other in many ways, including understanding the brain. Neuroscience studies the brain and nervous system, while psychology focuses on mental processes. By combining the two fields, researchers can better understand how the brain creates the mind. Neuroscience can help psychologists make more informed decisions about mental health treatments and interventions. For example, neurotherapy uses brain maps to identify physiological reasons for psychological feelings, and then retrain the brain. Neuroscience can help psychologists understand psychological concepts like memory and emotion. For example, the hippocampus is a key region in the brain that helps encode short-term memories into long-term memories. Neuropsychology studies how the brain and nervous system influence behaviour and cognition. Neuropsychology uses experimental and clinical research, as well as neuroimaging and standardised tests.

As an avid learner and student of science, I have always been fascinated by the complexities of the human brain. Neuroscience, the study of the nervous system and the brain, has been an area of interest for many scientists and researchers for centuries. If we are serious about preventing data breaches we should better understand neuroscience, the human

T. Singh, *Cybersecurity, Psychology and People Hacking*, Palgrave Studies in Cyberpsychology, https://doi.org/10.1007/978-3-031-85994-6_6

brain, how neuroscience is used in cybersecurity and the intersection of neuroscience and technology. Future development will involve neuroscience and artificial intelligence, the future of neuroscience, and advances in neuroscience research.

The history of neuroscience dates back to ancient civilisations. The Egyptians, for example, believed that the heart was the centre of thought and emotion. However, it was not until the Renaissance period that scientists began to study the human brain in detail. One of the most notable figures in the history of neuroscience was Leonardo da Vinci. He conducted numerous dissections of the human brain and made detailed sketches of its anatomy.

In the eighteenth and nineteenth centuries, there were significant advances in the field of neuroscience. Scientists such as Johannes Muller and Paul Broca made ground-breaking discoveries about the functions of different parts of the brain. These discoveries led to the development of new theories and models of brain function that are still used today.

The human brain is the most complex organ in the body. It consists of over 100 billion neurons, which are cells that transmit information throughout the nervous system. These neurons are connected by synapses, which are the points where information is transmitted between neurons.

The brain is divided into several different regions, each with its unique functions. For example, the frontal lobe is responsible for decision-making and problem-solving, while the temporal lobe is involved in memory and language processing. The brainstem and cerebellum are responsible for controlling vital functions such as breathing and balance.

As someone who has always been interested in the inner workings of the brain, I find the field of neuroscience to be absolutely fascinating. With advances in technology and research, we have been able to gain a better understanding of how the brain works and how it can be applied in various fields. One such field is cybersecurity, where the study of neuroscience has become increasingly important in recent years.

Neuroscience has numerous applications in the field of cybersecurity. One of the most significant uses is in the development of biometric authentication systems. Biometric authentication uses unique physical characteristics such as fingerprints or facial recognition to identify users.

This technology is becoming increasingly popular in the age of digital security threats.

Another area where neuroscience is used in cybersecurity is in the development of anti-phishing measures. Phishing attacks are a common tactic used by cybercriminals to steal sensitive information such as passwords and credit card details. By studying the way, the brain processes information, researchers can develop strategies to help users identify and avoid phishing attacks.

Neuroscience can help analyse the cognitive processes of pattern recognition, reasoning, and decision-making that are crucial in the detection and exploitation of security vulnerabilities. Understanding processes at a cognitive level helps to improve cybersecurity training. Neuroscience can also help understand the minds of cyberattackers and their thinking strategies both their heuristics and biases as well as their susceptibility to defensive techniques such as decoys or honeypots. Honeypots can be used to lure attackers into exploiting a dummy system containing misleading or false content. This can be valuable as it distracts cyberattackers from genuinely sensitive information and exhausts their limited time and resources.[1]

Neuroscience and its increased application with technology has led to numerous exciting developments in recent years. For example, brain-computer interfaces (BCIs) have the potential to revolutionise the way we interact with technology. BCIs allow users to control computers and other devices using their thoughts. This technology has numerous potential applications, from helping people with disabilities to improving gaming experiences.

Another area where neuroscience and technology intersect is in the development of virtual reality (VR) technology. VR technology can be used to create immersive experiences that simulate real-world environments. By studying the way the brain processes sensory information, researchers can design VR experiences that feel more realistic and engaging.

Artificial intelligence (AI) is another area where neuroscience has had a significant impact. Researchers have used insights from neuroscience to develop AI systems that can learn and adapt like humans. For example, deep learning algorithms are based on the structure of the human brain and are capable of recognising patterns and making predictions.

Another area where neuroscience is used in AI is in the development of natural language processing (NLP) systems. NLP systems are designed to understand and interpret human language. By studying the way the brain processes language, researchers can develop NLP systems that are more accurate and efficient.

Cyber neuroscience combines the principles of neuroscience and cybersecurity to better understand how the brain influences cyber behaviour. It involves the use of advanced tools and technologies to study the brain's responses to various cyber threats and how these responses can be used to improve cybersecurity measures.

Cybersecurity has become a crucial concern for individuals and organisations alike. With the increasing amount of sensitive information being stored online, it is more important than ever to ensure that our digital systems are secure. This is where the study of neuroscience comes in. By understanding how the brain works and how it responds to cyber threats, we can better predict and prevent potential cyberattacks.

Neuroscience plays a crucial role in cybersecurity by helping us understand how the human brain processes and responds to various cyber threats. By studying brain activity in response to these threats, we can better understand how to design effective cybersecurity measures that take into account the way our brains process information. This can help us create more secure systems that are less susceptible to cyberattacks.

There are several ways in which neuroscience can help improve cybersecurity. For example, by studying brain activity in response to phishing emails, we can better understand how to design emails that are less likely to be perceived as suspicious by the brain. Additionally, by studying the brain's response to various types of cyber threats, we can better predict and prevent potential attacks.

There are several key neuroscience concepts that are important for cybersecurity professionals to understand. One such concept is cognitive biases, which are inherent flaws in the way our brains process information. By understanding these biases, cybersecurity professionals can design systems that are less susceptible to social engineering attacks.

Another important concept is emotional arousal, which refers to the way our brains respond to emotional stimuli. By studying emotional arousal in response to cyber threats, we can better understand how to design systems that are less likely to trigger an emotional response in users.

Neuroscience research and innovation plays a key role in cybersecurity. There is currently a great deal of research being done in the field of cyber neuroscience. This research is focused on developing new tools and technologies that can be used to study the brain's response to various cyber threats. Additionally, there is a growing interest in using neuroscience to develop more effective cybersecurity measures, such as biometric authentication systems.

There are several tools and technologies that are used in the field of cyber neuroscience. One such technology is functional magnetic resonance imaging (fMRI), which is used to study brain activity in response to various stimuli. Another technology is electroencephalography (EEG), which is used to measure brain activity through the use of electrodes placed on the scalp.

Neuroscience plays a key role in understanding cyber behaviour. By studying the way our brains process information and respond to various stimuli, we can better understand why people behave the way they do online. This can help us design more effective cybersecurity measures that take into account the way our brains work.

By understanding how the brain works and how it responds to various cyber threats, we can better predict and prevent potential attacks. As technology continues to advance, we can expect to see even more innovation in this field, which will ultimately lead to more secure digital systems for everyone.

The future of neuroscience is full of exciting possibilities. Neuroscience is a fascinating field of study with numerous applications in diverse fields such as cybersecurity, technology, and medicine. As we continue to learn more about the human brain, we are likely to see even more exciting developments in the future. Whether it is the development of brain implants or the creation of more advanced AI systems, neuroscience is sure to play a significant role in shaping our future.

As technology continues to advance, the field of cyber neuroscience is likely to become even more important in the field of cybersecurity. We can expect to see more research and innovation in this area, as well as an increased focus on developing new tools and technologies that can be used to better understand the brain's response to cyber threats.

Sociology is the scientific study of social behaviour and human society. It is a discipline that focuses on understanding the patterns of human behaviour, social interactions, and the organisation of societies. Sociology is important because it helps us to better understand how society works, how people interact with each other, and how social issues arise. By analysing social phenomena, sociologists can identify problems and propose solutions to improve the lives of individuals and communities.

Psychology and sociology are both social sciences that study human behaviour, but they differ in their focus and approach. Psychology focuses on the individual, while sociology focuses on the group. Sociology examines broader societal structures, while social psychology focuses on individual behaviour and interactions within those structures.

The intersection of psychology and sociology is an emerging field that studies how social and psychological factors interact to shape human behaviour. Both fields are highly relevant in understanding behaviours in relation to cybersecurity.

Sociology deals with how people live and interact with each other, as well as how they shape and are shaped by the society in which they live. Sociology is an essential field of study because it helps us understand our world and the people in it. I will discuss the importance of Sociology, key concepts in Sociology, the evolution of Sociology, and the applications of Sociology in modern society. This is a broad field that encompasses a range of topics, including race, gender, class, culture, religion, and politics. Sociologists use a variety of research methods, including surveys, interviews, and observations, to study social behaviour. They also use statistical analysis to identify patterns and trends in social data.

Sociology has a rich history that dates back to the nineteenth century. The discipline emerged during a time of significant social and economic change, as the Industrial Revolution led to the growth of cities and the rise of capitalism. Early sociologists, such as Auguste Comte, Emile Durkheim, and Max Weber, sought to understand the social changes that were occurring and to develop theories to explain them.

Over time, sociology has evolved to include a wide range of perspectives and approaches. Contemporary sociologists draw on theories and concepts from a variety of fields, including psychology, anthropology, economics, and political science. The field has also become more interdisciplinary, with sociologists collaborating with experts in other fields to study complex social issues.

Sociology has a number of key theories and concepts that are used to study social behaviour. One of the most influential is the theory of social structure, which holds that social behaviour is shaped by the social institutions and organisations that exist within a society. Other important theories include socialisation, which explores how individuals develop their social identities, and social inequality, which examines the distribution of resources and power within a society.

Sociology is a vast field that encompasses many concepts. Some of the key concepts in Sociology include socialisation, culture, social stratification, social institutions, and deviance. Socialisation is the process by which individuals learn the values, norms, and behaviours of their society. Social norms are another important concept, as they dictate what is considered acceptable behaviour within a given social context. Culture refers to the beliefs, customs, practices, and material objects that make up a people's way of life. Social stratification is the organisation of society into layers based on wealth, power, and prestige. Social institutions are the established patterns of behaviour that provide stability and order in society, such as the family, education, and religion. Deviance refers to behaviour that is considered to violate the norms of a society.

Sociology as a discipline has evolved over time. It emerged in the early nineteenth century as a response to the social changes brought about by the Industrial Revolution. The early sociologists, such as Auguste Comte and Emile Durkheim, focused on the study of social order and how society could be studied scientifically. They believed that society was a complex system that could be understood through observation and analysis. In the twentieth century, Sociology became more diverse, with various schools of thought developing, including Functionalism, Conflict Theory, and Symbolic Interactionism.

Sociology has many applications in modern society. One of its most important applications is in the study of social problems. Sociologists study issues such as poverty, inequality, and discrimination, and develop solutions to these problems. Sociology also has applications in business, where it is used to study consumer behaviour and market trends. In the field of healthcare, Sociology is used to study the social factors that influence health and illness. Sociologists also study crime and deviance, and their research is used to develop policies and programmes aimed at reducing crime rates.

Technology has played an increasingly important role in sociology in recent years. Advances in computer technology and data analysis have made it possible for sociologists to collect and analyse large amounts of social data. This has led to the development of new research methods and techniques, such as social network analysis and machine learning.

Technology has also had an impact on the way that sociologists communicate and collaborate. The internet has made it easier for researchers to share data and findings across geographic boundaries, and social media platforms have provided new opportunities for public engagement and outreach.

In recent years, there has been an increasing intersection between Sociology and Cybersecurity. Cybersecurity refers to the protection of computer systems and networks from unauthorised access or attack. The role of Sociology in Cybersecurity is to understand the social factors that contribute to cyber threats and develop strategies to mitigate them. Sociologists have identified a number of social factors that contribute to cyber threats, including the digital divide, social engineering, and online radicalisation.

Sociology plays a crucial role in Cybersecurity. Sociologists study the social factors that contribute to cyber threats, such as social engineering and online radicalisation. They develop strategies to mitigate these threats, such as educating users on safe online practices and developing policies to prevent cyberbullying. For example, we know adolescents involved in experiences of cybervictimisation and cyberbullying are at increased risk of psychological maladjustment and ill-being.[2] However, not all adolescents involved in cyberbullying roles experience this and cognitive emotion regulation (CER) might be a key factor. Sociologists are helping research how CER strategies could help with cyberbullying behaviour, and there could be some predictive utility of these strategies in predicting cybervictimisation and cyberbullying. It is crucial that cybersecurity professionals and sociologists work together on this problem as we know children and adolescents are less likely to disclose cyber victimisation but self-disclosure is an important coping strategy to reduce future incidences of cyber victimisation.[3] This highlight the complexity of this in terms of gender and nature of social support. If we don't tackle this complex social problem we risk a future where maladjusted youngsters escalate negative behaviours.

Sociologists work with Cybersecurity professionals to develop effective Cybersecurity strategies that take into account the social factors that contribute to cyber threats. Sociology has an important role to play. Cybersecurity is a complex and rapidly evolving field that requires a deep understanding of both technology and human behaviour. Sociologists can contribute to cybersecurity by studying the social and cultural factors that influence cyber behaviour. For example, sociologists can examine the social norms and values that drive individuals to engage in cybercrime and identify strategies for changing those norms and values. They can also study the social dynamics of cyberattacks, such as the ways in which attackers communicate and collaborate with one another.

The impact of sociology on cybersecurity is already being felt. Sociological research has contributed to the development of new cybersecurity strategies and technologies, such as behavioural biometrics and social engineering awareness training. Sociologists have also helped to identify gaps in existing cybersecurity policies and procedures, and to develop strategies for addressing those gaps.

In addition, sociology has helped to raise awareness about the importance of addressing social and cultural factors in cybersecurity. By highlighting the role that social norms, values, and institutions play in shaping cyber behaviour, sociologists have helped to shift the focus of cybersecurity from purely technical solutions to a more holistic approach that takes into account the human element.

Cyber sociology is a subfield of sociology that focuses specifically on the study of social behaviour in online environments. It examines the ways in which people interact with one another online, and the social structures and institutions that exist within those environments.

Cyber sociology is an important field because it helps us to better understand the social dynamics of online communities and the ways in which they shape our behaviour. It can also help us to identify strategies for promoting positive social interactions online and mitigating the negative effects of online behaviour.

Sociology plays a crucial role in understanding and preventing Cybercrime. Cybercrime refers to criminal activities that are carried out using computer networks or the internet. Sociologists study the social factors that contribute to Cybercrime, such as the digital divide and online radicalisation. They also work with law enforcement agencies to develop effective strategies for preventing Cybercrime and prosecuting Cybercriminals.

Cybercrime and cyberattacks are complex social phenomena that require a sociological approach to understand. Sociologists can help to identify the social and cultural factors that drive individuals to engage in cybercrime, and to develop strategies for preventing and addressing cyberattacks.

For example, sociologists can examine the social norms and values that make cybercrime more or less acceptable within particular communities and develop interventions to change those norms and values. They can also study the social dynamics of cyberattacks, such as the ways in which attackers communicate and collaborate with one another, and develop strategies for disrupting those networks.

To understand the sociology of cybercrime, we need to understand the social context and the social structures that enable cybercrime. Cybercriminals are not just individuals, but they operate within social networks and are influenced by social factors. For example, the Ashley Madison Hack was not just a case of individual hackers, but it was enabled by the social context of a website that enabled infidelity. Similarly, the WannaCry Ransomware Attack was enabled by the social context of outdated software and a lack of cybersecurity measures.

Sociology also helps us understand the motivations of cybercriminals. Cybercrime is not just about money, but it can also be about revenge, activism, or even terrorism. Understanding the motivations of cybercriminals can help us develop better strategies for preventing cybercrime.

Case Study: The Ashley Madison Hack

The Ashley Madison Hack was a data breach that occurred in 2015, where hackers stole data from the website Ashley Madison, which was a dating site for people who were married or in a relationship. The hackers threatened to release the data unless the website was shut down. The data included personal information such as names, addresses, and credit card information.[4]

From a sociology perspective, the Ashley Madison Hack was enabled by the social context of a website that enabled infidelity. The website created a social structure that allowed people to engage in infidelity, which made it a target for hackers. Moreover, the social stigma associated with infidelity made it difficult for the victims to report the crime or seek help.

Case Study: The WannaCry Ransomware Attack

The WannaCry Ransomware Attack was a global cyberattack that occurred in May 2017. The attack targeted computers running the Microsoft Windows operating system by encrypting data and demanding ransom payments in the form of Bitcoin. The attack affected over 200,000 computers in 150 countries.

The WannaCry Ransomware Attack was enabled by the social context of outdated software and a lack of cybersecurity measures. Many of the affected computers were running outdated software that was vulnerable to the attack. Moreover, many organisations did not have adequate cybersecurity measures in place to prevent the attack.

Case Study: The Target Data Breach

The Target Data Breach was a data breach that occurred in 2013, where hackers stole data from the retailer Target. The data included personal information such as names, addresses, and credit card information. The hackers used malware to gain access to Target's payment system.

The Target Data Breach was enabled by the social context of a lack of cybersecurity measures. Target did not have adequate cybersecurity measures in place to prevent the attack. Moreover, the social structure of the retail industry created a system where retailers were responsible for securing their own payment systems, which made it difficult to detect and prevent the attack.

Cybercrime has a significant impact on society. The victims of cybercrime can suffer financial losses, identity theft, and emotional distress. Moreover, cybercrime can have broader social consequences, such as undermining trust in institutions and damaging the economy.

Cybercrime also has a disproportionate impact on vulnerable populations, such as the elderly and low-income individuals. These populations may be more susceptible to cybercrime and may be less able to recover from the financial losses.

Sociology plays an important role in preventing cybercrime. By understanding the social context and the social structures that enable cybercrime, we can develop better strategies for preventing cybercrime. For example, by addressing the social stigma associated with infidelity, we may be able to reduce the demand for websites like Ashley Madison. By promoting cybersecurity measures in organisations, we can reduce the vulnerability of our systems to cyberattacks.

Moreover, sociology can help us understand the broader social consequences of cybercrime. By understanding the impact of cybercrime on society, we can develop better policies and regulations to prevent cybercrime and mitigate its impact.

Sociology can provide valuable insights into the sociology of cybercrime. By understanding the social context and the social structures that enable cybercrime, we can develop better strategies for preventing cybercrime. The case studies of The Ashley Madison Hack, The WannaCry

Ransomware Attack, and The Target Data Breach illustrate how sociology can help us understand the social factors that enable cybercrime. By addressing these social factors, we can reduce the vulnerability of our systems to cyberattacks and mitigate the impact of cybercrime on society.

There are several sociological approaches to Cybersecurity. One approach is to study the social factors that contribute to cyber threats and develop strategies to mitigate them. Another approach is to study the social effects of Cybersecurity policies and programmes. For example, how does Cybersecurity affect privacy and civil liberties? Sociologists also study the social impacts of Cybercrime, such as the emotional and financial effects on victims.

The Sociology of Cybersecurity risks is concerned with understanding the social factors that contribute to Cybersecurity risks. These factors include the digital divide, social engineering, online radicalisation, and the human factor. The human factor refers to the fact that humans are often the weakest link in Cybersecurity, as they can be tricked into revealing sensitive information or downloading malware.

As technology continues to advance and permeate every aspect of our lives, the need for sociological research and analysis will only increase. Sociologists will continue to play an important role in cybersecurity, as they work to understand the social and cultural factors that drive cyber behaviour and develop strategies for addressing those factors.

In addition, sociology will continue to evolve and adapt to new technological developments, such as the rise of artificial intelligence and the internet of things. Sociologists will work to understand the social implications of these technologies and to develop policies and strategies to ensure that they benefit society as a whole.

Sociology is an important discipline that helps us to better understand how society works and how social issues arise. In the context of cybersecurity, sociology is particularly important, as it helps us to understand the social and cultural factors that drive cyber behaviour and to develop strategies for addressing those factors. As technology continues to advance, the need for sociological research and analysis will only increase, and sociologists will continue to play an important role in shaping the future of cybersecurity.

Cybersecurity threats will become more complex and sophisticated. Sociologists will play an important role in understanding these threats and developing strategies to mitigate them. As society becomes more dependent on technology, the intersection of Sociology and Cybersecurity will become even more important.

Sociology is an essential field of study that helps us understand our world and the people in it. It has many applications in modern society, including the study of social problems, business, healthcare, and crime. The intersection of Sociology and Cybersecurity is becoming increasingly important as technology continues to advance. Sociologists play a crucial role in understanding the social factors that contribute to Cybersecurity threats and developing strategies to mitigate them. The future of Sociology in Cybersecurity is promising, and we can expect to see continued growth in this field in the years to come.

Anthropology concerns the scientific study of human beings, their cultures, and societies. It is a broad and interdisciplinary field that draws on theories and methods from sociology, psychology, biology, and other social sciences. The discipline of anthropology has a long and fascinating history that spans thousands of years, from the early days of human civilisation to the present.

Psychology and anthropology are both relevant to cybersecurity and intersect in several ways, including through the subfield of psychological anthropology and through cross-cultural psychology. Psychological anthropology is the subfield of anthropology that studies how psychological factors interact with culture, and how culture influences individuals. It examines topics like personality, memory, and mental illness, but focuses on how these phenomena are influenced by culture. Psychological anthropologists use methods like participant observation and qualitative interviews to study these topics.

Cross-cultural psychology focuses on understanding how human behaviour varies across cultures. Cross-cultural psychologists use the comparative method to identify universals in human behaviour.

Interpretive anthropology is a mode of anthropological inquiry that was influenced by psychologists' ideas about patterns and configuration. Anthropology provides the broader cultural context, while psychology provides insights into individual and group behaviour within that context. Anthropology can help us understand why people experience mental distress, and what well-being and happiness might look like.

The origins of anthropology can be traced back to the ancient Greek philosopher Aristotle, who wrote about the diversity of human societies and cultures. However, the formal study of anthropology did not begin until the nineteenth century, when European explorers and colonial administrators began to document the cultures and customs of the peoples they encountered in the Americas, Africa, and Asia.

The first anthropologists were primarily interested in the classification and comparison of different cultures and societies. They sought to identify the features that were common to all human societies, as well as the unique characteristics of each. This approach, known as cultural evolutionism, was based on the assumption that all societies progressed through a series of stages of development, from simple to complex.

In the early twentieth century, anthropology underwent a major shift, as scholars began to reject the idea of cultural evolution and instead focused on the study of individual cultures and societies in their own right. This approach, known as cultural relativism, emphasised the need to understand each culture on its own terms, without imposing external standards or judgements.

Today, anthropology is a highly diverse and interdisciplinary field, encompassing a broad range of subfields, including biological anthropology, linguistic anthropology, and cultural anthropology.

Anthropology is a complex and multifaceted field that encompasses a broad range of topics and methodologies. At its core, anthropology is concerned with understanding human beings and their cultures and societies. This involves studying everything from the biological and genetic factors that shape human behaviour to the social, political, and economic systems that underpin human societies.

One of the key strengths of anthropology is its ability to take a holistic and interdisciplinary approach to understanding human behaviour. Anthropologists use a wide range of research methods, including ethnography, participant observation, interviews, and surveys, to collect data about human cultures and societies. They also draw on theories and methods from other disciplines, such as sociology, psychology, and biology, to develop a comprehensive understanding of human behaviour.

Anthropology is also notable for its emphasis on cultural relativism, which recognises that each culture is unique and must be understood on its own terms. This approach emphasises the importance of avoiding ethnocentrism, or the tendency to judge other cultures based on one's own cultural norms and values.

In recent years, the field of anthropology has become increasingly important in the context of cybersecurity. As our lives become increasingly interconnected and our reliance on digital technologies grows, the need to understand the social and cultural dimensions of cybersecurity has become more pressing.

One of the key challenges facing cybersecurity professionals is the need to address the human factors that contribute to cyber threats. This includes understanding the motivations and behaviours of cyber criminals, as well as the social and cultural factors that shape these behaviours.

Anthropology is uniquely positioned to help address these challenges, as it provides a framework for understanding the complex interactions between technology, culture, and society. By studying the social and cultural factors that drive cyber threats, anthropologists can help identify the root causes of cybercrime and develop more effective strategies for preventing and addressing these threats.

Anthropology has a growing role in the field of cybersecurity. One of the primary areas where anthropology is making an impact is in the development of more effective cybersecurity policies and practices.

For example, anthropologists are working with cybersecurity professionals to develop more effective training programmes that address the social and cultural factors that contribute to cyber threats. By understanding the motivations and behaviours of cyber criminals, these programmes can help users become more aware of potential threats and develop better strategies for protecting themselves and their organisations.

Anthropologists are also working to develop more effective strategies for addressing cybercrime. By understanding the social and cultural factors that drive cybercrime, anthropologists can help identify the root causes of these threats and develop more effective strategies for preventing and addressing them.

The role of anthropology in cybersecurity is multifaceted. Anthropologists bring a unique perspective to cybersecurity challenges, as they are trained to understand the complex interactions between technology, culture, and society.

One of the key roles of anthropology in cybersecurity is to help identify the social and cultural factors that drive cyber threats. By studying the motivations and behaviours of cyber criminals, anthropologists can help develop more effective strategies for preventing and addressing these threats.

Anthropologists also play a key role in developing more effective cybersecurity policies and practices. By working with cybersecurity professionals to develop more effective training programmes and strategies, anthropologists can help ensure that users are better equipped to protect themselves and their organisations.

Anthropology can improve cybersecurity in a number of ways. One of the primary ways is by providing a more comprehensive understanding of the social and cultural factors that contribute to cyber threats.

By studying the motivations and behaviours of cyber criminals, anthropologists can help develop more effective strategies for preventing and addressing these threats. They can also help identify the root causes of cybercrime, and develop more effective policies and practices for addressing these threats.

Anthropology can also help improve cybersecurity by providing a more nuanced understanding of the human factors that contribute to cyber threats. By studying the social and cultural factors that shape user behaviour, anthropologists can help develop more effective training programmes and strategies for promoting better cybersecurity practices.

Anthropology has an important role to play in understanding and addressing cybercrime. Cybercrime is a complex and multifaceted phenomenon that involves a wide range of social, cultural, and technological factors.

Anthropologists can help to shed light on the social and cultural factors that drive cybercrime, and develop more effective strategies for preventing and addressing these threats. By studying the motivations and behaviours of cyber criminals, anthropologists can help identify the root causes of cybercrime and develop more effective policies and practices for addressing these threats.

There are a number of examples that highlight the important role that anthropology can play in cybersecurity. One example is the use of ethnographic research to study the motivations and behaviours of cyber criminals.

By conducting in-depth interviews and participant observation with cyber criminals, anthropologists can gain a better understanding of the social and cultural factors that drive cybercrime. This can help inform the development of more effective cybersecurity policies and practices that are better tailored to the specific needs and motivations of cyber criminals.

Another example is the use of anthropological research to develop more effective training programmes for cybersecurity professionals. By studying the social and cultural factors that shape user behaviour, anthropologists can help identify the most effective strategies for promoting better cybersecurity practices.

Anthropology offers a unique perspective on cyberattacks, as it allows us to examine the complex cultural and social factors that contribute to these attacks. By studying the behaviours and motivations of cyberattackers, we can gain insights into how they think and operate. Additionally, anthropology can help us understand the cultural context in which cyberattacks occur, such as political and economic conditions, social norms, and power dynamics.

One of the primary benefits of using anthropology to understand cyberattacks is that it can help us identify patterns and trends in these attacks. For example, by analysing the language and symbols used by cyberattackers, we can gain insights into their cultural background and beliefs. This information can be used to develop more effective strategies for preventing and responding to cyberattacks.

Case Study 1: The Target Data Breach

The Target data breach, which occurred in 2013, is one of the most significant cyberattacks in recent history. The attack resulted in the theft of over 40 million credit and debit card numbers, as well as other personal information. Anthropologists have studied this attack to gain insights into the motivations and behaviours of the attackers.

One of the key findings of these studies is that the attackers were highly organised and sophisticated. They used a combination of social engineering and technical skills to gain access to Target's systems. Additionally, the attackers appeared to be motivated by financial gain, rather than political or ideological reasons.

Case Study 2: The Equifax Data Breach

The Equifax data breach, which occurred in 2017, is another example of the significant impact of cyberattacks. The breach resulted in the theft of personal information for over 143 million people. Anthropologists have studied this attack to gain insights into the cultural and social factors that contributed to this breach.

One of the key findings of these studies is that the Equifax breach was the result of a combination of technical vulnerabilities and organisational failures. Additionally, the breach highlighted the significant power imbalances between consumers and large corporations, as well as the challenges in regulating the cybersecurity industry.

Case Study 3: The WannaCry Ransomware Attack

The WannaCry ransomware attack, which occurred in 2017, is a prime example of the potential impact of cyberattacks on critical infrastructure. The attack targeted healthcare systems, financial institutions, and other critical infrastructure, causing significant disruption and financial loss. Anthropologists have studied this attack to gain insights into the motivations and behaviours of the attackers.

One of the key findings of these studies is that the WannaCry attack was likely the work of a nation-state actor, rather than a criminal organisation. Additionally, the attack highlighted the significant vulnerabilities in critical infrastructure systems, as well as the need for more effective communication and collaboration between public and private sector organisations.

Anthropological studies of cyberattacks have highlighted the critical role of cultural factors in these attacks. For example, cultural norms around privacy and trust can contribute to the success or failure of social engineering attacks. Additionally, cultural beliefs about the role of technology in society can influence the motivations of cyberattackers.

Another critical cultural factor in cyberattacks is power dynamics. Cyberattacks often occur in the context of broader power struggles, such as geopolitical conflicts or economic competition. Understanding these power dynamics is critical for developing effective strategies for preventing and responding to cyberattacks.

Anthropologists have developed several approaches to cybersecurity that highlight the importance of interdisciplinary collaboration and cultural sensitivity. One such approach is the concept of 'cyber cultures', which emphasises the need to understand the cultural and social context in which cyberattacks occur.

Another approach is the concept of 'security cultures', which highlights the importance of developing a culture of security within organisations. This approach emphasises the need to promote security awareness and education among employees, as well as the need to develop effective policies and procedures for preventing and responding to cyberattacks.

Anthropologists have also developed several solutions to the challenges of cybersecurity. One such solution is the concept of 'red teaming', which involves simulating cyberattacks to identify vulnerabilities and develop effective countermeasures. Another solution is the use of cultural sensitivity training for cybersecurity professionals, which can help them better understand the cultural context in which cyberattacks occur.

Additionally, anthropologists have emphasised the importance of interdisciplinary collaboration in developing effective cybersecurity solutions. By working with experts from other fields, such as computer science and psychology, anthropologists can develop more comprehensive and effective approaches to cybersecurity.

Anthropology case studies in cybersecurity highlight the critical role of cultural and social factors in these attacks. By studying these factors, anthropologists can gain insights into the motivations and behaviours of cyberattackers, as well as the cultural context in which these attacks occur. Additionally, anthropology offers several approaches and solutions to the challenges of cybersecurity, emphasising the importance of interdisciplinary collaboration and cultural sensitivity.

As cyberattacks continue to pose significant threats to individuals and organisations, it is critical that we take an interdisciplinary approach to cybersecurity. By working together and leveraging the insights of anthropology and other fields, we can develop more effective strategies for preventing and responding to cyberattacks.

As our reliance on digital technologies continues to grow, the need for a more comprehensive understanding of the social and cultural dimensions of cybersecurity will only become more pressing.

In the coming years, we can expect to see a greater emphasis on interdisciplinary research that draws on the insights and methods of anthropology, sociology, psychology, and other social sciences. We can also expect to see a greater focus on developing more effective strategies for addressing the human factors that contribute to cyber threats.

Overall, the role of anthropology in cybersecurity is critical to ensuring that we are able to develop more effective policies and practices for protecting ourselves and our organisations in the digital age.

Anthropology is a complex and multifaceted field that has an increasingly important role to play in the field of cybersecurity. By providing a more comprehensive understanding of the social and cultural factors that drive cyber threats, anthropologists can help develop more effective strategies for preventing and addressing these threats. We will continue to develop more interdisciplinary approaches to understanding human behaviour and technology. By working together, cybersecurity professionals and anthropologists can help ensure that we are better equipped to protect ourselves and our organisations in the digital age.

Notes

1. Krawczyk, D., Bartlett, J., Kantarcioglu, M., Hamlen, K., & Thuraisingham, B. (2013). Measuring expertise and bias in cyber security using cognitive and neuroscience approaches. In *2013 IEEE International Conference on Intelligence and Security Informatics,* pp. 364–367.
2. Quintana-Orts, C., Mérida-López, S., Rey, L., Chamizo-Nieto, M. T., & Extremera, N. (2023). Understanding the role of emotion regulation strategies in cybervictimization and cyberaggression over time: It is basically your fault! *Cyberpsychology: Journal of Psychosocial Research on Cyberspace, 17*(2), Article 1. https://doi.org/10.5817/CP2023-2-1
3. Salton, M. R., Cohen, R., Deptula, D. P., & Ray, G. E. (2023). Willingness to self-disclose cyber victimization to friends or parents: Gender differences in cyber victimization a year later. *Cyberpsychology: Journal of Psychosocial Research on Cyberspace, 17*(2), Article 2. https://doi.org/10.5817/CP2023-2-2
4. Cross, C., Parker, M., & Sansom, D. (2019). Media discourses surrounding 'non-ideal' victims: The case of the Ashley Madison data breach. *International Review of Victimology, 25*(1), 53–69. https://doi.org/10.1177/0269758017752410

7

Social Engineering: Exploiting Human Psychology

As technology continues to evolve, so do the tactics that cybercriminals use to gain access to sensitive information. Social engineering is one of the most common tactics used by hackers to exploit human behaviour for cyberattacks. We can consider what social engineering is, the psychology behind it, the types of social engineering attacks, examples of social engineering attacks, the impact of social engineering on cybersecurity, how to identify and mitigate social engineering risks, trust, authority, and social norms in social engineering, social engineering prevention strategies, and best practices for cybersecurity awareness.

Social engineering involves the use of psychological manipulation to influence individuals into divulging confidential information or performing actions that are not in their best interest. It involves the exploitation of human behaviour, emotions, and trust to gain access to sensitive information. Social engineering is a form of cyberattack that relies heavily on human interaction rather than technical exploits. It is a type of attack that targets the weakest link in the security chain – humans.

Social engineering tactics work by appealing to basic human emotions and needs such as fear, greed, curiosity, and trust. These tactics are designed to take advantage of the natural human tendency to trust and

T. Singh, *Cybersecurity, Psychology and People Hacking*, Palgrave Studies in Cyberpsychology, https://doi.org/10.1007/978-3-031-85994-6_7

help others. Social engineers often use pretexting, baiting, phishing, and other tactics to manipulate people into divulging sensitive information or performing actions that are not in their best interest.

Pretexting involves creating a fake scenario or pretext to gain a victim's trust. For example, a social engineer may pose as a bank representative and ask a victim to divulge their account details. Baiting involves enticing the victim with an offer or reward in exchange for sensitive information. For example, a social engineer may offer a free gift card in exchange for the victim's credit card details. Phishing involves sending fake emails or messages that appear to be from a legitimate source to trick the victim into divulging confidential information.

There are many different types of social engineering attacks that cybercriminals use to exploit human behaviour. The most common types of social engineering attacks include phishing, spear phishing, baiting, pretexting, and watering hole attacks.

Phishing attacks involve sending a fake email or message that appears to be from a legitimate source to trick the victim into divulging sensitive information. Spear phishing attacks are similar to phishing attacks, but they are more targeted and personalised for specific victims. Attackers may target those in an organisation with privileged access such as those in IT or potential victims that have high access to sensitive data such as those in Human Resources or Finance functions. Baiting attacks involve enticing the victim with an offer or reward in exchange for sensitive information. Pretexting attacks involve creating a fake scenario or pretext to gain the victim's trust. Whaling is a form of spear phishing in which the attacker targets higher-value targets, such as executives in the C-Suite. Attacks such as business email compromise (BEC) make extensive use of it. Watering hole attacks involve compromising a popular website or online resource that the victim is likely to visit.

Business Email Compromise (BEC) is a key area of compromise. BEC attacks usually go unnoticed by cybersecurity teams, so they require specific awareness training to be prevented.

There are three main types of BEC social engineering attacks:

1. Impersonation. This occurs when scammers use spoof emails to pose as employees or trusted vendors and clients. They'll ask their target to send fraudulent payments, change payroll and direct deposit information, or share sensitive information.
2. Account compromise. This occurs when hackers gain access to a legitimate employee email address. Scammers can reply to and send emails company-wide (to clients, vendors, etc.), containing malicious code.
3. Thread hijacking. This is an advanced take on an account compromise attack. Thread hijacking occurs when hackers scan compromised inboxes for subject lines containing 'Re:'. They then automatically reply with malware-laced messages. Recipients open the hacked email, not thinking twice because they 'know' the sender.

Honeytraps (romance scams) are a type of romance scam in which scammers create fake online dating and social media profiles using attractive stolen photos. For example, in a military romance scam, the fraudster will pose as an active service member stationed far away and unable to meet in person. Once they identify a target, they'll start sending flirty and provocative messages, and quickly tell their victims they're in love with them. But they need the victims to prove they feel the same way by sending gifts, cash, or cryptocurrency. Honeytraps are especially rampant on social media sites like Snapchat. Honeytraps are also used to compromise employees in order to gain access to infrastructure.

Social engineering attacks are based on the principles of human psychology. Cybercriminals use various psychological techniques to manipulate their targets into divulging sensitive information or performing actions that compromise security. For example, they may use authority to convince their targets that they have the power to make changes to their accounts or systems. They may also use urgency to make their targets feel that they need to act quickly to avoid negative consequences.

Social engineering attackers use various techniques to manipulate their targets into divulging sensitive information or performing actions that compromise security. These techniques include building rapport, trust, creating a sense of urgency, appealing to authority, and using emotional appeals. For example, attackers may build rapport by pretending to be a friend or colleague and engaging in small talk before asking for sensitive information.

Social engineering attacks are becoming more sophisticated, and attackers are using new techniques to trick their targets. For example, attackers may use deepfake technology to create fake videos that appear to be from a trusted source. They may also use voice cloning technology to impersonate someone's voice over the phone. Another example of a social engineering attack is a CEO fraud, where an attacker impersonates a CEO or other high-level executive and requests sensitive information or a wire transfer.

Social engineering attacks can have a significant impact on individuals and organisations. When attackers gain access to sensitive information or systems, they can cause financial loss, reputational damage, and legal issues. Individuals may experience identity theft, financial loss, or damage to their reputation. Organisations may lose revenue, face legal action, or suffer damage to their reputation. Social engineering attacks can also cause significant disruption to operations and lead to downtime.

Scareware is the practice of tricking victims into believing that their system is afflicted with malware by using false alarms and fabricated threats. This leads them to install software that helps the threat actor, either to spread malware or obtain information. Scareware can be anything from pop-ups and notifications to basic spam emails.

A straightforward social engineering technique called tailgating is utilised to physically enter an unapproved area. The criminal follows the victim into the area undetected in order to accomplish this.

Similar to tailgating, piggybacking occurs when the victim lets the attacker use their credentials. The attacker does this by taking advantage of human emotions like kindness or empathy. For someone posing as a new employee who has lost her access badge, the victim would hold a secure door open.

Requesting the exchange of private information in return for a service that the attacker provides to the victim is known as the quid pro quo technique. For instance, a criminal may telephone a computer user and offer to increase connectivity while impersonating as their IT service provider.

Dumpster diving is the practice of searching trash cans for private information before it has been destroyed.

Similar to classic phishing, SMS phishing, also known as smishing, uses instant messaging apps and SMS rather than emails. Phishing campaigns are increasingly being launched by threat actors using channels other than emails.

Similar to smishing or email phishing, social media phishing involves communicating via social media sites. Although LinkedIn and Twitter messages are very popular for reaching professionals, many of us are also accustomed to receiving phoney messages on Facebook, Instagram, and TikTok.

Voice phishing, often known as vishing, is a social engineering approach in which the threat actor calls the target rather than emails them in an attempt to obtain private information or grant them remote access to their computer. They mimic speech patterns that the sufferer has never used.

Social engineering attacks have been used to target individuals, businesses, and government organisations. Some of the most notable social engineering attacks include the Target data breach, the RSA security breach, and the Office of Personnel Management data breach.

In the Target data breach, cybercriminals used a phishing email to gain access to the company's network. They were able to steal sensitive information from millions of customers. In the RSA security breach, cybercriminals used a spear phishing attack to gain access to the company's network. They were able to steal sensitive information related to the company's security products. In the Office of Personnel Management data breach, cybercriminals used a watering hole attack to compromise the agency's network. They were able to steal sensitive information related to government employees.

Social engineering attacks are becoming increasingly common and are having a significant impact on cybersecurity. Cybercriminals are using social engineering tactics to gain access to sensitive information, steal identities, and commit fraud. The impact of social engineering on cybersecurity is far-reaching and can result in significant financial losses, reputational damage, and legal liability.

Identifying and mitigating social engineering risks is essential for protecting against cyberattacks. It is important to be aware of the tactics that cybercriminals use to exploit human behaviour and to implement security measures that can help prevent these types of attacks. Some of the most effective ways to identify and mitigate social engineering risks include employee training, security awareness programmes, and implementing security policies and procedures.

Trust, authority, and social norms play a significant role in social engineering attacks. Cybercriminals often use these factors to gain the victim's trust and manipulate their behaviour. Social engineering attacks are often successful because the victim is not aware of the tactics that cybercriminals use or is not aware that they are being targeted.

There are many different strategies that can be used to prevent social engineering attacks. Some of the most effective strategies include employee training, implementing security policies and procedures, using two-factor authentication, and implementing security awareness programmes.

Employee training is essential for preventing social engineering attacks. Employees should be trained on the tactics that cybercriminals use and how to identify and report suspicious behaviour. Implementing security policies and procedures can also help prevent social engineering attacks. These policies should include guidelines for handling sensitive information, password policies, and guidelines for responding to security incidents.

Implementing best practices for cybersecurity awareness is essential for protecting against social engineering attacks. Some of the best practices for cybersecurity awareness include using strong passwords, avoiding public Wi-Fi, keeping software up to date, and using antivirus software.

Social engineering is a type of cyberattack that relies heavily on human interaction rather than technical exploits. It is a form of cyberattack that targets the weakest link in the security chain – humans. Understanding the psychology behind social engineering and implementing effective prevention strategies is essential for protecting against these types of attacks. By implementing best practices for cybersecurity awareness and being aware of the tactics that cybercriminals use, individuals and organisations can mitigate the risks associated with social engineering attacks.

8

Case Studies: Social Engineering Tactics

Over a career of over 20 years, I have seen first-hand the devastating effects that social engineering attacks can have on individuals and organisations. Social engineering is a technique that hackers use to manipulate people into giving up confidential information or performing actions that compromise security. I have seen how social engineering has been used to breach even the most secure systems. Social engineering attacks are often designed to exploit human vulnerabilities, like trust or fear, to trick individuals into divulging sensitive information or taking actions that compromise an organisation's security. We can consider some real-life case studies of social engineering attacks and provide some tips for avoiding them. I will share real-life case studies of social engineering attacks that have been used to breach cybersecurity.

Social engineering relies on psychological manipulation rather than technical skills. Hackers use social engineering tactics to exploit human vulnerabilities and trick people into divulging sensitive information or performing actions that compromise security. Social engineering attacks can take many forms, including phishing emails, pretexting, baiting, and quid pro quo.

T. Singh, *Cybersecurity, Psychology and People Hacking*, Palgrave Studies in Cyberpsychology, https://doi.org/10.1007/978-3-031-85994-6_8

Phishing emails are one of the most common types of social engineering attacks. In a phishing attack, a hacker sends an email that appears to be from a legitimate source, such as a bank or a social media platform, and asks the recipient to click on a link or provide personal information. Pretexting is another type of social engineering attack where the hacker creates a false identity to gain access to sensitive information. Baiting involves leaving a physical device, such as a USB drive, in a public place in the hopes that someone will pick it up and plug it into their computer. Quid pro quo is a type of social engineering attack where the hacker promises a reward, such as a gift card, in exchange for sensitive information.

Case Study 1: The Bangladesh Bank Heist

In February 2016, hackers stole $81 million from the Bangladesh Bank in what is considered one of the largest bank heists in history.[1] The hackers used a combination of social engineering tactics, including phishing emails and pretexting, to gain access to the bank's computer systems. The hackers created fake identities and used them to send emails to the bank's employees, asking for login credentials. Once they had access to the bank's systems, the hackers transferred money to accounts in the Philippines and Sri Lanka.

Case Study 2: The Snapchat Breach

In 2014, hackers gained access to the personal information of 4.6 million Snapchat users, including usernames, phone numbers, and email addresses.[2] The hackers used a combination of phishing emails and pretexting to trick Snapchat employees into giving up their login credentials. Once they had access to the system, the hackers downloaded the user data and posted it online.

Case Study 3: The BitPaymer Ransomware Attack

In 2019, the City of Edcouch, Texas, fell victim to a BitPaymer ransomware attack.[3] The hackers used a combination of phishing emails and baiting to gain access to the city's computer systems. The hackers sent an email to an employee of the city's public works department, posing as a job applicant and attaching a resume. The resume contained a malicious file that, when opened, installed the ransomware on the city's systems. The city was forced to pay a ransom of $35,000 to regain access to their data.

Case Study 4: The GoDaddy Phishing Attack

In March 2021, an employee of GoDaddy, a web hosting company, fell victim to a phishing attack that resulted in the compromise of several cryptocurrency exchanges. The hackers created a fake GoDaddy login page and sent the employee a phishing email asking them to log in to their account. Once the employee entered their login credentials, the hackers had access to the GoDaddy account and were able to change the DNS settings for several cryptocurrency exchanges, redirecting users to a fake website that stole their login credentials.

Case Study 5: The Google and Facebook Phishing Scam

In 2017, a Lithuanian man named Evaldas Rimasauskas was arrested for orchestrating a phishing scam that targeted two tech giants, Google and Facebook. Rimasauskas created a fake company and sent phishing emails to employees of the two companies, tricking them into wiring him over $100 million.[4]

The phishing emails were designed to look like legitimate business emails from a vendor that the companies regularly worked with. The emails contained fake invoices and contracts that requested payment to a bank account controlled by Rimasauskas. The emails were well-crafted and appeared to be legitimate, fooling even the most security-savvy employees.

This case demonstrates how social engineering attacks can be highly sophisticated and difficult to detect, as attackers can use social engineering techniques to manipulate individuals into taking actions that put their organisations at risk.

Case Study 6: The Tesla Twitter Hack

In 2020, a group of hackers targeted Tesla CEO Elon Musk's Twitter account as part of a social engineering attack. The hackers gained control of Musk's account and used it to tweet out a bitcoin scam. The scam involved a promise to double any bitcoin payments sent to a specific wallet address.

The hackers used social engineering tactics to lure victims into sending bitcoin to the scam address. They relied on the trust that individuals had in Elon Musk's account to make the scam appear legitimate. The scam was successful, and the hackers were able to steal over $100,000 worth of bitcoin.[5]

This case demonstrates how social engineering attacks can be used to exploit trusted individuals, like celebrities or business leaders, to gain access to sensitive information or steal money.

Case Study 7: The Carbanak Group's Bank Heist

The Carbanak group is a Russian cybercrime gang that is responsible for one of the largest bank heists in history. The group used social engineering tactics to gain access to the networks of over 100 banks in 40 countries, stealing over $1 billion.

The group used phishing emails to trick bank employees into downloading malware onto their computers. Once the malware was installed, the group was able to gain access to the bank's internal systems and steal money. The group also used social engineering tactics to trick bank employees into transferring money to fake accounts controlled by the group.[6]

This case demonstrates how social engineering attacks can be used to steal large amounts of money from financial institutions. The attacks were successful because the group was able to use social engineering tactics to bypass the banks' security measures and gain access to sensitive information.

Case Study 8: The W-2 Tax Form Scam

In 2016, cybercriminals used a social engineering attack to steal the tax information of over 120,000 employees from Seagate Technology. The attackers sent phishing emails to Seagate employees that appeared to be from a senior executive in the company. The emails requested that the employees send the W-2 tax forms of all employees to a specified email address.[7]

The employees believed that the email was legitimate and sent the sensitive tax information to the attackers. The attackers were able to use this information to file fraudulent tax returns and steal money from the victims.

This case demonstrates how social engineering attacks can be used to steal sensitive information, like tax and financial information, from organisations. The attackers were successful because they were able to use social engineering tactics to manipulate the employees into sending the sensitive information.

Case Study 9: The DNC Email Hack

In 2016, the Democratic National Committee (DNC) was the target of a social engineering attack that led to the theft of thousands of emails. The attackers used phishing emails to trick DNC employees into divulging their email credentials. Once the attackers had access to the email accounts, they were able to steal sensitive information and leak it to the public.

The attackers used social engineering tactics to make the phishing emails appear legitimate. They designed the emails to look like they came from Google, warning the employees that their email accounts had been compromised and that they needed to change their passwords immediately. The employees believed the emails were legitimate and provided their credentials, allowing the attackers to gain access to their email accounts.[8]

This case demonstrates how social engineering attacks can be used to steal sensitive information and manipulate public opinion. The attackers were successful because they were able to use social engineering tactics to make their phishing emails appear legitimate and exploit the trust that the employees had in their email provider.

Social engineering attacks are becoming increasingly common and sophisticated. The case studies I have shared demonstrate how social engineering tactics can be used to bypass even the most advanced security measures. To protect against social engineering attacks, organisations need to educate their employees about the risks and provide regular training on how to identify and avoid social engineering attacks.

Implementing password-less or multi-factor authentication, limiting access to sensitive information, and regularly testing security measures can also help protect against social engineering attacks. By taking proactive measures to protect against social engineering attacks, organisations can reduce the risk of a breach and protect their sensitive information from being stolen or leaked.

There are simple tips that individuals and organisations can follow to avoid falling victim to social engineering attacks. First, it is important that all employees and users are made more aware of the different types of social engineering tactics and to be sceptical of any unsolicited emails or messages. Second, it is important to follow the principle of least privilege by limiting access to information to only those who really need it in order to protect sensitive information. Third, it is important to keep software and systems up to date with the latest security patches to minimise vulnerabilities.

In addition to these simple tips, individuals and organisations can also invest in more sophisticated security awareness training to educate employees about social engineering tactics and how to avoid them. Simulated phishing attacks can also be used to test employees' awareness and to identify areas for improvement.

Social engineering attacks are a serious threat to cybersecurity that can have devastating consequences. By understanding the different types of social engineering tactics and following best practice for avoiding them, individuals and organisations can take steps to protect themselves from these types of attacks.

Notes

1. https://www.wired.com/2016/05/insane-81m-bangladesh-bank-heist-heres-know/
2. https://www.twingate.com/blog/tips/snapchat-data-breach
3. https://www.pcrisk.com/removal-guides/12859-bitpaymer-ransomware
4. https://cyberscoop.com/facebook-google-scam-man-sentenced/
5. https://www.dfs.ny.gov/Twitter_Report
6. https://www.europol.europa.eu/media-press/newsroom/news/mastermind-behind-eur-1-billion-cyber-bank-robbery-arrested-in-spain
7. https://www.trendmicro.com/vinfo/gb/security/news/cybercrime-and-digital-threats/seagate-employees-face-possible-tax-fraud-in-recent-phishing-attack
8. https://edition.cnn.com/2016/12/26/us/2016-presidential-campaign-hacking-fast-facts/index.html

9

Interview with a Cyberattack Victim

What follows is a transcript from a broader interview that was conducted between the author and the victim of a cyberattack. They asked for their identity to be changed so that they are protected from any further cyberattacks as their personal information has been leaked previously.

Author: Thank you for agreeing to this interview. Let's start with your experience. Can you describe what happened during the cyberattack?

Victim: Sure. It all started one morning when I couldn't log into my email. At first, I thought it was just a technical glitch. But then, I realised my social media accounts were compromised too. It was terrifying to realise that someone had invaded my personal and professional space.

Author: That sounds incredibly stressful. How did the realisation affect you emotionally?

Victim: It was like a nightmare. My first reaction was panic. I felt violated, and there was a profound sense of helplessness. It wasn't just the loss of my data but the fear of what the hacker might do with my personal information. I had sleepless nights and constant anxiety. The psychological toll was immense.

Author: I can only imagine. How did it impact your daily life and relationships?

T. Singh, *Cybersecurity, Psychology and People Hacking*, Palgrave Studies in Cyberpsychology, https://doi.org/10.1007/978-3-031-85994-6_9

Victim: The constant fear of being watched or exploited was overwhelming. I became overly cautious and paranoid. Simple things like opening an email or logging into a website triggered anxiety. I also found it hard to trust people, even those close to me. It strained my relationships because I was always on edge.

Author: That sounds incredibly isolating. What about your professional life? How did the cyberattack affect your career?

Victim: Professionally, it was a disaster. As a freelance consultant, my reputation is everything. The hacker sent malicious emails from my accounts, which hurt my clients and business relationships. I had to spend countless hours rebuilding my online presence, securing my accounts, and reassuring my clients. The financial impact was significant, but the damage to my credibility was even worse.

Author: It sounds like you had to rebuild from scratch. What steps did you take to recover?

Victim: The recovery process was long and painful. I worked with cybersecurity experts to secure my accounts and systems. I also had to communicate openly with my clients about the situation. Therapy played a crucial role in helping me cope with the psychological impact. Gradually, I started to regain my confidence, but the scars remain.

Author: You mentioned therapy being a crucial part of your recovery. Can you elaborate on how it helped you deal with the psychological aftermath?

Victim: Therapy was essential. It provided a safe space to express my fears and frustrations. My therapist helped me understand that my reactions were normal for someone who had been through such a traumatic experience. We worked on strategies to manage my anxiety and rebuild my sense of security. It was a gradual process, but it made a significant difference in my mental health.

Author: Did you experience any long-term psychological effects?

Victim: Yes, unfortunately. Even though I've regained a lot of my confidence, I still have moments of paranoia. For instance, I often question the security of my devices and sometimes feel anxious when I receive emails from unknown senders. There's also a lingering fear of it happening again, which can be quite overwhelming at times.

Author: It sounds incredibly challenging. Did you notice any changes in your behaviour or personality because of the attack?

Victim: Definitely. Before the attack, I was very open and trusting. The cyberattack made me more cautious and sceptical. It also impacted my social interactions; I started avoiding social gatherings and became more withdrawn. Trusting others, even family and friends, became difficult because I felt constantly on guard.

Author: It's heartbreaking to hear how deeply this has affected you. How did you manage your day-to-day activities during the height of your anxiety?

Victim: It was tough. I had to adopt a routine that included regular breaks to avoid feeling overwhelmed. Mindfulness exercises and meditation became a part of my daily life. They helped me stay grounded and present. I also made sure to stay connected with supportive friends and family who understood what I was going through.

Author: That's a resilient approach. What impact did the cyberattack have on your sense of identity and self-worth?

Victim: The attack shook my sense of identity to its core. It felt like my personal space, my very essence, had been violated. I questioned my judgement and decision-making skills—how did I let this happen? There was a lot of self-blame initially. Over time, with professional help and support from loved ones, I started to rebuild my self-worth. I realised that the blame lay with the attacker, not me.

Author: It's inspiring to see how you've turned a traumatic experience into a journey of resilience and recovery. What message would you like to send to others who might be going through a similar ordeal?

Victim: First and foremost, don't blame yourself. The fault lies with the attacker, not the victim. Reach out for support, whether it's from friends, family, or professionals. And remember, it's okay to feel vulnerable and to seek help. The journey to recovery might be long, but with time and support, you can regain your strength and confidence.

Author: Given everything you've been through, what advice would you give to others to protect themselves from similar attacks?

Victim: Prevention is key. Use strong, unique passwords for different accounts, and enable two-factor authentication wherever possible. Stay informed about the latest cybersecurity threats and practices. Most importantly, don't hesitate to seek professional help, both technical and psychological, if you become a victim. It's crucial to address both the digital and emotional damage.

Author: Thank you for sharing your story. I hope it helps others understand the gravity of cyberattacks and take necessary precautions.

Victim: Thank you for giving me the platform to share my experience. If my story can help even one person avoid what I went through, it's worth it.

10

Interview with a CISO

What follows is a transcript from a broader interview that was conducted between the author and an experienced Chief Information Security Officer (CISO) in a business in a highly regulated sector.

Author: Thank you for taking the time to speak with me. As a CISO, you have a critical role in ensuring the security of your organisation. Can you start by explaining what a typical day looks like for you?

CISO: Of course. My day usually begins with reviewing the latest security updates and any overnight incidents. I then meet with my team to discuss our priorities and any new threats. Much of my day involves collaborating with different departments to ensure our security protocols are being followed and addressing any vulnerabilities we might find. It's a constant cycle of monitoring, assessing risks, and implementing solutions.

Author: It sounds intense. What are some of the biggest challenges you face in your role?

CISO: One of the biggest challenges is staying ahead of the ever-evolving threat landscape. Cyber criminals are always developing new methods to breach defences, so we have to be proactive and innovative in our approach. Another challenge is balancing security with usability. We

T. Singh, *Cybersecurity, Psychology and People Hacking*, Palgrave Studies in Cyberpsychology, https://doi.org/10.1007/978-3-031-85994-6_10

need to protect our systems without hindering the productivity of our employees.

Author: That's definitely a delicate balance. Can you tell us about a time when your organisation faced a significant cyber threat, and how you handled it?

CISO: Certainly. There was an incident last year where we detected unusual activity on our network. It turned out to be a sophisticated phishing attack that had compromised several employee accounts. We immediately isolated the affected systems and launched an investigation. Our team worked around the clock to contain the breach, secure our network, and restore affected services. We also conducted a thorough review of our security measures and implemented additional safeguards to prevent a recurrence.

Author: That must have been quite a stressful situation. What strategies do you employ to ensure your team is prepared to handle such threats?

CISO: Training and continuous education are key. We conduct regular simulations and drills to keep our team sharp and ready to respond to incidents. We also invest in the latest security technologies and ensure our team is well-versed in how to use them. Collaboration with other organisations and sharing threat intelligence is also crucial for staying informed about new and emerging threats. We talk about mental health in our 1:1s and as a group.

Author: How do you keep up with the rapid advancements in technology and the increasing sophistication of cyber threats?

CISO: It's a combination of staying informed and being adaptable. We attend industry conferences, participate in webinars, and read the latest research and reports. Networking with other professionals in the field is also invaluable. Adaptability is crucial; we must be willing to adjust our strategies and adopt new technologies as they become available.

Author: Cybersecurity often seems like a constant battle. What motivates you to stay in this field despite the challenges?

CISO: The sense of purpose and responsibility is a major motivator. Knowing that my work helps protect the organisation and its stakeholders from significant harm is incredibly fulfilling. I also enjoy the challenge and the need to stay on my toes. The field of cybersecurity is dynamic and constantly evolving, which keeps things exciting and engaging.

Author: That's an admirable perspective. What advice would you give to aspiring cybersecurity professionals?

CISO: My advice would be to stay curious and never stop learning. The field is constantly changing, and there's always something new to discover. Gain as much hands-on experience as possible, whether through internships, labs, or personal projects. Networking is also important—connect with others in the field and learn from their experiences. And remember, security is a team effort, so collaboration and communication skills are just as important as technical expertise. Dedicate time to discuss mental health as part of team and individual development discussions.

Author: It's clear that being a CISO involves a lot of responsibility and stress. Can you talk about the psychological toll that comes with the job?

CISO: Absolutely. The role of a CISO is inherently high-pressure. We're always on alert, knowing that any lapse in security could have severe consequences for the organization. The constant vigilance and the weight of that responsibility can be mentally exhausting. There's also the pressure of staying ahead of cyber threats, which evolve rapidly. This means long hours and a never-ending learning curve.

Author: That sounds incredibly demanding. How do you cope with the stress and maintain your mental health?

CISO: It's a challenge, no doubt. I've found that maintaining a work-life balance is crucial, even though it's easier said than done. Regular physical exercise, mindfulness practices, and having a supportive network of colleagues, friends, and family are essential. Taking time to disconnect and recharge is important, too. It helps me stay focused and effective in my role.

Author: It must be tough to find that balance. Have you noticed any specific signs of burnout in yourself or your team?

CISO: Yes, burnout is a significant risk in this field. Signs include chronic fatigue, irritability, and a decreased ability to concentrate. In myself, I notice it when I start feeling overwhelmed by tasks that I usually handle with ease. It's crucial to recognize these signs early and take proactive steps to address them, such as delegating tasks, taking short breaks, and seeking support from peers or mental health professionals.

Author: You've mentioned burnout as a significant risk in your role. Can you describe how ongoing burnout affects you personally?

CISO: The effects of ongoing burnout are profound. It's not just about feeling tired; it's a deep sense of physical and emotional exhaustion. There are days when even the simplest tasks feel overwhelming. This constant state of stress can also lead to health issues, such as headaches, insomnia, and even more serious conditions like high blood pressure. Mentally, it can make you feel detached and indifferent, which is dangerous in a role that requires constant vigilance and proactive decision-making.

Author: That sounds incredibly challenging. How does burnout manifest within your team?

CISO: Within the team, burnout can lead to decreased morale and productivity. When team members are constantly stressed, they're more likely to make mistakes, which can be costly in the cybersecurity field. There's also an increase in absenteeism and turnover, as people struggle to cope with the relentless demands of the job. It's a vicious cycle because as more people leave or take time off, the remaining team members have to pick up the slack, which only exacerbates the problem.

Author: It seems like a never-ending cycle. What steps have you taken to address burnout in your team?

CISO: We've implemented several measures to help manage and mitigate burnout. Firstly, we've increased the frequency of mental health check-ins and encourage open discussions about stress and workload. We've also introduced more flexible working hours and ensure that team members take regular breaks. Additionally, we provide access to professional mental health resources and encourage everyone to take advantage of them. Lastly, we're working on improving workload distribution to ensure no one is overwhelmed.

Author: It's great to see those proactive steps. Have these measures had a noticeable impact on your team?

CISO: Yes, they have. While burnout is still a challenge, we've seen improvements in team morale and productivity. Open communication has helped normalise conversations about mental health, which has been crucial. Flexible working hours and better workload management have also allowed team members to find a better work-life balance, which is essential for long-term sustainability.

Author: Given the high stakes of your job, how do you motivate your team to stay engaged and committed?

CISO: Motivation in such a high-pressure environment often comes from a sense of purpose and belonging. We make sure to highlight the importance of each team member's role in protecting our organisation and its stakeholders. Recognizing and rewarding hard work is also crucial. Whether through formal acknowledgments or simple thank-you notes, showing appreciation goes a long way. We also foster a collaborative environment where everyone feels valued and supported.

Author: What advice would you give to other leaders in high-stress fields to help manage their own burnout and that of their teams?

CISO: Prioritize mental health and well-being just as much as you prioritise meeting objectives. Regularly check in with yourself and your team, and be open to discussing stress and workload. Lead by example by taking breaks and setting boundaries for work hours. Encourage a culture where taking care of mental health is seen as a strength, not a weakness. Invest in professional support and resources, and make sure they are easily accessible to everyone.

Author: How does the constant exposure to potential threats and incidents affect your mental outlook?

CISO: It can lead to a sense of hyper-vigilance and sometimes even paranoia. The nature of our work means we have to anticipate and think like attackers, which can alter our perception of the digital world. This hyper-awareness can seep into personal life, making it difficult to switch off and relax. It's a double-edged sword—being highly alert helps us do our jobs well, but it also takes a toll on mental health.

Author: Given the high stakes, do you find that the job impacts your personal relationships?

CISO: Yes, it can. The stress and long hours can sometimes make it challenging to be fully present in personal relationships. Communication is key; explaining the nature of the job to loved ones helps them understand the demands and stress involved. It's also important to set boundaries to ensure that work doesn't encroach on personal time.

Author: What advice would you give to other CISOs or cybersecurity professionals to help them manage the psychological demands of the job?

CISO: Prioritise self-care and mental health just as you would with physical health. Seek support when needed, whether through peer networks, professional counselling, or stress management programmes. Encourage open communication within your team about mental health and stress. Also, invest in personal development outside of work to create a well-rounded life that can buffer the pressures of the job.

Author: It's encouraging to hear that even in such a high-stress role, there are ways to manage the psychological impact. Any final thoughts for our readers?

CISO: Just to remember that cybersecurity is a marathon, not a sprint. The landscape is always evolving, and while the challenges are significant, so are the rewards. Taking care of your mental health is crucial for sustaining a long and successful career in this field.

Author: Thank you for your openness and insights. It's clear that the work you do is incredibly important, and your dedication to both your role and your well-being is inspiring.

CISO: Thank you for the opportunity to share my experiences. It's important to discuss these issues openly, and I hope it encourages others to take care of their mental health as seriously as they take their cybersecurity responsibilities.

11

Interview with a Convicted Hacker

What follows is a transcript from a broader interview that was conducted between the author and a former hacker who was convicted after serious and well-publicised cyberattacks. They asked for their identity to be changed so that they are protected from any further legal implications. Hence hereon we refer to them by the pseudonym Shadow.

Shadow's most daring hacks included:

Corporate Espionage: Shadow infiltrated a major tech company's network to steal proprietary information about an upcoming product. This involved bypassing multiple layers of security, including advanced firewalls and intrusion detection systems. The stolen data was sold to a competitor, causing significant financial and reputational damage to the original company.

Financial Institution Breach: In one of his most high-stakes operations, Shadow managed to hack into a large bank's internal systems. He accessed sensitive customer data and financial records, which he used to siphon off small amounts of money from thousands of accounts. The amounts were small enough to go unnoticed initially, but collectively, they added up to a substantial sum.

T. Singh, *Cybersecurity, Psychology and People Hacking*, Palgrave Studies in Cyberpsychology, https://doi.org/10.1007/978-3-031-85994-6_11

Government Database Hack: Shadow once targeted a government database containing personal information of millions of citizens. This hack required not only technical expertise but also social engineering skills to manipulate insiders into providing access. The data was used to create fake identities and commit various forms of fraud.

Ransomware Attack: Shadow deployed a sophisticated ransomware attack on a multinational corporation. He encrypted critical data and demanded a hefty ransom in cryptocurrency. The company, unable to operate without the data, was forced to pay the ransom. This attack highlighted the vulnerability of even the most well-protected systems to ransomware.

Public Infrastructure Sabotage: In a particularly bold move, Shadow hacked into the control systems of a city's public transportation network. He disrupted services, causing chaos and significant economic impact. This hack was a demonstration of his capabilities and a warning to other potential targets.

These hacks demonstrate Shadow's technical prowess, strategic planning, and ability to exploit both technological and human vulnerabilities. Each operation required meticulous preparation and execution, reflecting his evolution from a curious teenager to a highly skilled and dangerous hacker.

Author: Thank you for agreeing to this interview. Can you start by telling us a bit about yourself and how you got into hacking?

Hacker: Sure. I go by the alias 'Shadow'. I started hacking when I was a teenager, mostly out of curiosity. I was fascinated by computers and how they worked. Over time, I realised I had a knack for it and began exploring more complex systems.

Author: What motivated you to start hacking businesses specifically?

Hacker: Initially, it was the challenge. Breaking into secure systems gave me a thrill. But as I got older, I saw opportunities to make money. Businesses often have valuable data, and there are buyers willing to pay a lot for it.

Author: Can you describe a typical hacking operation?

Hacker: It usually starts with reconnaissance. I gather as much information as possible about the target. This includes employee details, network structure, and any vulnerabilities. Then, I use various tools and techniques to exploit these weaknesses and gain access to their systems.

Author: What kind of data do you typically target?

Hacker: It varies. Sometimes it's financial data, other times it's intellectual property or customer information. Anything that can be sold or used for blackmail is valuable.

Author: How do you stay anonymous and avoid getting caught?

Hacker: I use a combination of techniques. This includes using encrypted communication channels, masking my IP address, and using multiple layers of proxies. I also avoid leaving any digital footprints that can be traced back to me.

Author: Have you ever had any close calls with law enforcement?

Hacker: A few times. There have been moments when I thought they were onto me, but I managed to cover my tracks. It's a constant game of cat and mouse.

Author: Do you ever feel guilty about the impact your actions have on businesses and their customers?

Hacker: Sometimes. I know what I do can cause a lot of harm. But I try to justify it by telling myself that these businesses should have better security. If I can get in, so can others with worse intentions.

Author: Shadow, you've shared a lot about your activities and motivations. Can you delve deeper into your psychology? What drives you to hack, and how do you cope with the pressures of living a double life?

Hacker: That's a deep question. At the core, my journey into hacking started with pure curiosity. I was fascinated by how systems work and the challenge of breaking into them. It's like solving a complex puzzle, and the satisfaction of cracking it is immense.

Author: So, it's the intellectual challenge that drives you?

Hacker: Partly, yes. But it's more than that. There's a thrill, an adrenaline rush that comes with each successful hack. The risk, the challenge, the sense of power—it's addictive. Knowing that I can outsmart sophisticated security systems gives me a sense of control and superiority.

Author: How do you reconcile this with the potential harm your actions cause?

Hacker: That's something I struggle with. I try to justify it by telling myself that I'm exposing vulnerabilities that need to be fixed. If I can get in, so can others with worse intentions. But, honestly, there are moments when I feel guilty, especially when I see the real-world impact of my actions.

Author: Living a double life must be stressful. How do you manage that?

Hacker: It's incredibly stressful. I have to be constantly vigilant, always on guard to avoid detection. It's a lonely existence because I can't share this part of my life with anyone. The fear of getting caught is always there, and it takes a toll. I try to compartmentalise my life, keeping my hacking activities separate from my personal life. But it's not easy.

Author: Does this isolation affect your relationships?

Hacker: Definitely. Maintaining secrecy strains my relationships. Friends and family don't know what I do, so there's always a barrier. It's hard to form genuine connections when you're hiding such a big part of your life.

Author: How do you cope with the emotional strain?

Hacker: I engage with online communities of like-minded individuals. It helps to talk to people who understand what I'm going through. I also try to rationalise my actions to alleviate guilt. But the emotional strain is always there, lurking in the background.

Author: Thank you for sharing this, Shadow. It gives a lot of insight into the psychological complexities of being a hacker.

Hacker: You're welcome. It's a complicated life, but it's the path I've chosen.

Author: Thank you for agreeing to be part of this. I appreciate this must have been difficult and I'm grateful that you shared your views. Hopefully this may help provide the readers some insight into the mindset of hackers and help them to understand some of the root causes.

This conversation highlighted the intricate blend of motivations and the psychological toll that comes with living a double life as a hacker. Shadow's reflections provide a deeper understanding of the internal conflicts and coping mechanisms that define his existence.

Shadow's motivations seemed to be multifaceted and evolved over time. Initially, his interest in hacking stemmed from a deep curiosity and a desire to understand how computer systems work. This curiosity quickly turned into a passion for the challenge of breaking into secure systems, which provided a significant adrenaline rush.

As Shadow's skills developed, he began to see the financial opportunities that hacking presented. The ability to access valuable data and sell it on the black market became a strong motivator. This shift from curiosity to financial gain marked a significant turning point in his hacking career.

However, Shadow's motivations are not purely financial. There's also a sense of power and control that comes from being able to infiltrate and manipulate systems that are supposed to be secure. This feeling of being able to outsmart sophisticated security measures can be very intoxicating.

Despite these motivations, Shadow is not entirely devoid of a moral compass. He sometimes justifies his actions by pointing out the flaws in the security systems of businesses, believing that if he can exploit these weaknesses, others with more malicious intent could do the same. This rationalisation helps him cope with any guilt he might feel about the harm his actions cause.

Overall, Shadow's motivations are a complex mix of curiosity, financial gain, the thrill of the challenge, and a desire for power and control, tempered by occasional moments of self-justification and moral reflection.

Shadow employed a variety of sophisticated techniques to maintain his anonymity during his hacking operations. A few examples are provided below:

Use of Proxies and VPNs: Shadow routed his internet traffic through multiple proxy servers and Virtual Private Networks (VPNs) to mask his IP address. This made it difficult for anyone to trace his activities back to his actual location.

Tor Network: For added anonymity, Shadow often used the Tor network, which encrypts and routes internet traffic through a series of volunteer-operated servers around the world. This further obscured his digital footprint.

Encrypted Communication: All of Shadow's communications were encrypted using strong encryption protocols. He used secure messaging apps and email services that offered end-to-end encryption to ensure that his conversations could not be intercepted or read by unauthorised parties.

Disposable Devices: Shadow frequently used disposable devices, such as burner phones and laptops, which he would discard after completing a hack. This prevented any physical device from being linked back to him.

Virtual Machines and Sandboxes: He conducted his hacking activities within virtual machines and sandbox environments. This isolated his activities from his main operating system, reducing the risk of leaving traces that could be used to identify him.

Social Engineering: Shadow was adept at social engineering, which involved manipulating people into divulging confidential information. By gaining access through human vulnerabilities, he often avoided the need to directly hack into systems, thereby reducing his digital footprint.

Regularly Changing Tactics: To stay ahead of law enforcement and cybersecurity experts, Shadow constantly changed his tactics and tools. This made it difficult for anyone to develop a consistent profile or pattern of his activities.

No Personal Identifiers: Shadow was meticulous about not leaving any personal identifiers in his hacking activities. He avoided using personal accounts, names, or any information that could be linked back to his real identity.

By combining these techniques, Shadow was able to operate under the radar and avoid detection, making it extremely challenging for authorities to track him down.

Shadow's psychology is a complex blend of curiosity, thrill-seeking, and a desire for control, tempered by occasional moral reflections. Here are some key aspects:

Curiosity and Intelligence: Shadow's journey into hacking began with a deep-seated curiosity about how systems work. This intellectual curiosity drives him to constantly learn and adapt, staying ahead of security measures and evolving his techniques.

Thrill-Seeking: The adrenaline rush from successfully breaching secure systems is a significant motivator. Each hack presents a new challenge, and the excitement of overcoming these challenges keeps Shadow engaged and motivated.

Desire for Control: Hacking gives Shadow a sense of power and control. Being able to manipulate and access systems that are designed to be secure provides a feeling of superiority and mastery over technology.

Financial Motivation: Over time, financial gain became a strong motivator. The ability to monetise his skills by selling stolen data or demanding ransoms adds a practical, albeit illegal, incentive to his activities.

Moral Ambiguity: Shadow experiences moments of moral reflection. He justifies his actions by pointing out the security flaws in the systems he breaches, believing that his hacks expose vulnerabilities that could be exploited by others with worse intentions. This rationalisation helps him cope with any guilt.

Isolation and Anonymity: The need to stay anonymous and avoid detection leads to a solitary lifestyle. Shadow operates in isolation, which can contribute to a sense of detachment from the real-world consequences of his actions.

Strategic Thinking: Successful hacking requires meticulous planning and strategic thinking. Shadow's ability to plan and execute complex operations reflects a highly analytical and strategic mindset.

Adaptability: The constantly evolving nature of cybersecurity means that Shadow must be highly adaptable. He continuously updates his knowledge and techniques to stay ahead of security measures and law enforcement.

Ethical Flexibility: While Shadow occasionally reflects on the ethical implications of his actions, his primary focus remains on the challenge and rewards of hacking. This ethical flexibility allows him to navigate the moral grey areas of his activities.

Overall, Shadow's psychology is characterised by a blend of intellectual curiosity, thrill-seeking, a desire for control, and financial motivation, all balanced by a complex and sometimes contradictory moral framework.

The psychology of hackers like Shadow is quite intricate and involves factors that drive them to extreme lengths. Here's a deeper look into their motivations and the psychological toll of living a double life:

Shadow's motivations can be summed up as:

Curiosity and Intellectual Challenge: Many hackers are driven by a deep curiosity and a desire to understand and manipulate complex systems. The intellectual challenge of bypassing security measures and solving intricate problems is a significant motivator.

Thrill and Adrenaline: The act of hacking can provide a significant adrenaline rush. The risk involved and the satisfaction of successfully breaching a secure system can be highly addictive.

Desire for Power and Control: Hacking gives individuals a sense of power and control over systems and data. This can be particularly appealing to those who feel powerless or marginalised in other areas of their lives.

Financial Gain: The potential for financial rewards is a strong motivator. Selling stolen data, demanding ransoms, or engaging in corporate espionage can be highly lucrative.

Recognition and Status: Within the hacking community, successful hacks can earn respect and recognition. This sense of belonging and status can be a powerful incentive.

Moral Justification: Some hackers justify their actions by believing they are exposing vulnerabilities that need to be addressed. They may see themselves as ethical hackers or vigilantes, despite the illegal nature of their activities.

Psychological toll on Shadow includes:

Constant Vigilance: Living a double life requires constant vigilance. Hackers must always be on guard to avoid detection, which can lead to chronic stress and anxiety.

Isolation: To maintain anonymity, hackers often operate in isolation. This can lead to feelings of loneliness and detachment from society.

Moral Conflict: Even if they rationalise their actions, hackers may still experience guilt or moral conflict, especially if their actions cause significant harm. This internal conflict can manifest in many different ways.

Fear of Consequences: The fear of being caught and facing legal consequences is a constant source of stress. This fear can be exacerbated by high-profile arrests and crackdowns on cybercrime.

Dual Identity Strain: Balancing a normal life with a secret hacking identity can be mentally exhausting. The need to compartmentalise different aspects of their lives can lead to cognitive dissonance and emotional strain.
Impact on Relationships: Maintaining secrecy can strain personal relationships. Friends and family may be unaware of the hacker's activities, leading to a lack of genuine connection and support.

To manage these psychological challenges, hackers like Shadow develop various coping mechanisms:

Compartmentalisation: Keeping their hacking activities separate from their personal lives to manage stress and maintain a sense of normalcy.
Community Support: Engaging with online communities of like-minded individuals for support and validation.
Rationalisation: Justifying their actions to alleviate guilt and maintain a positive self-image.
Mindfulness and Stress Management: Some may adopt techniques like mindfulness or other stress management practices to cope with the pressures of their double life.

Understanding the psychology of hackers like Shadow helps to shed light on the complex interplay of motivations and the significant psychological toll of living a double life.

12

Interview with a People Hacker (Social Engineering)

What follows is a transcript from a broader interview that was conducted between the author and a people hacker who was highly prolific with increasingly high-profile targets. They asked for their identity to be changed so that they are protected from any further legal implications. Hence hereon we refer to them by a pseudonym.

Author: Thank you for agreeing to this interview. To start, can you tell us a bit about yourself and how you got into social engineering?

Hacker: Absolutely. I go by the alias 'ShadowFox'. My journey into social engineering began in my teenage years. I was always fascinated by human behaviour and the psychology behind decision-making. Combining that with my interest in technology, social engineering became a natural fit.

Author: That's intriguing. Can you explain what social engineering is for those who might not be familiar?

Hacker: Social engineering is essentially the art of manipulating people into giving up confidential information. It involves exploiting human psychology rather than technical hacking techniques. This could be through phishing emails, pretexting, baiting, or even physical impersonation.

T. Singh, *Cybersecurity, Psychology and People Hacking*, Palgrave Studies in Cyberpsychology, https://doi.org/10.1007/978-3-031-85994-6_12

Author: What was your first successful social engineering hack?

Hacker: My first major success was during my college years. I managed to gain access to a professor's email account by posing as an IT support technician. I convinced him that his account had been compromised and that I needed his credentials to secure it. It was a simple yet effective tactic.

Author: How do you choose your targets?

Hacker: I usually target businesses with weak security protocols and high-value data. I start by gathering as much information as possible about the company and its employees. LinkedIn, social media, and company websites are gold mines for this kind of information.

Author: Can you share a particularly memorable hack?

Hacker: One of the most memorable was infiltrating a mid-sized financial firm. I created a fake LinkedIn profile posing as a new employee in the IT department. Over a few weeks, I built rapport with several employees and eventually convinced one of them to give me access to the company's internal network. From there, I was able to extract sensitive financial data.

Author: That's quite a story. What do you think makes social engineering so effective?

Hacker: The effectiveness lies in its simplicity. People are often the weakest link in any security system. No matter how advanced the technology, if you can manipulate a person into giving you access, you can bypass most security measures. Trust and authority are powerful tools in social engineering.

Author: Have you ever felt conflicted about your actions?

Hacker: There are definitely moments of reflection. I understand the impact my actions can have on individuals and businesses. However, I also see it as a way to highlight vulnerabilities and push for better security practices. In some cases, I've even been hired by companies to test their defences.

Author: What advice would you give to businesses to protect themselves against social engineering attacks?

Hacker: Education and awareness are key. Regular training for employees on recognising and responding to social engineering tactics is crucial.

Implementing strict verification processes for sensitive information and encouraging a culture of scepticism can also go a long way.

Author: ShadowFox, you've shared some fascinating stories about your exploits. I'm curious, what motivates you to engage in social engineering hacking?

Hacker: That's a great question. My motivations have evolved over time. Initially, it was the thrill of the challenge and the intellectual satisfaction of outsmarting systems. There's a certain adrenaline rush that comes with successfully executing a complex social engineering scheme.

Author: So it started as a personal challenge. Has that changed over the years?

Hacker: Yes, definitely. As I gained more experience, I began to see the broader implications of my actions. I realised that by exposing vulnerabilities, I could actually help improve security practices. In some ways, it's become a mission to raise awareness about the importance of cybersecurity and the human element in it.

Author: That's an interesting perspective. Do you ever work with organisations to help them strengthen their defences?

Hacker: Absolutely. I've transitioned into a role where I often work as a security consultant. Companies hire me to test their defences through simulated social engineering attacks. It's a way to use my skills for good and contribute to a safer digital environment.

Author: It sounds like you've found a way to balance your skills with a positive impact. What keeps you motivated now?

Hacker: The landscape of cybersecurity is always changing, and that keeps things exciting. There's always something new to learn and new challenges to tackle. Plus, knowing that my work can help prevent real harm to businesses and individuals is a strong motivator.

Author: Do you have any long-term goals or aspirations in this field?

Hacker: Long-term, I hope to continue advocating for better security practices and perhaps even mentor the next generation of cybersecurity professionals. There's a lot of talent out there, and guiding them towards ethical hacking and security consultancy can make a big difference.

Author: That's admirable. Before we wrap up, is there any final advice you'd like to give to our readers?

Hacker: Stay informed and vigilant. Cybersecurity isn't just the responsibility of IT departments; it's something everyone needs to be aware of. Educate yourself about common social engineering tactics and always verify before you trust.

Author: ShadowFox, you've mentioned the impact of your work and your evolving motivations. Have you ever faced any ethical dilemmas in your career as a social engineering hacker?

Hacker: Definitely. Ethical dilemmas are almost inevitable in this line of work. One of the biggest challenges is balancing the thrill of the hack with the potential consequences for the people and organisations involved. Early on, I didn't always consider the full impact of my actions.

Author: Can you give an example of a specific ethical dilemma you've encountered?

Hacker: Sure. There was a time when I gained access to a healthcare provider's system. I had the ability to access sensitive patient information, and while my initial intent was to demonstrate the vulnerabilities, I realised the potential harm if that information were to be misused. It was a wake-up call about the responsibility that comes with this kind of access.

Author: How did you handle that situation?

Hacker: I decided to report the vulnerabilities directly to the organisation without exploiting the data. It was a turning point for me, reinforcing the importance of ethical considerations in my work. Since then, I've made it a point to ensure that my actions, even when testing security, do not cause harm.

Author: It sounds like that experience had a significant impact on you. How do you navigate these ethical boundaries now?

Hacker: I adhere to a strict personal code of ethics. I always ask myself whether my actions could cause harm and whether they align with my goal of improving security. When in doubt, I err on the side of caution. Additionally, working as a consultant has provided a framework where my activities are authorised and intended to help organisations.

Author: Have you ever turned down a job because of ethical concerns?

Hacker: Yes, there have been a few instances where I felt the client's intentions were not aligned with ethical practices. For example, if a company wanted me to hack a competitor or engage in activities that felt more like corporate espionage than security testing, I declined. It's important to maintain integrity in this field.

Author: That's commendable. What advice would you give to others in the cybersecurity field regarding ethics?

Hacker: Always prioritise the well-being of individuals and organisations over personal gain or the thrill of the hack. Establish a clear ethical framework for your work and stick to it. Remember that with great power comes great responsibility, and our actions can have far-reaching consequences.

Author: ShadowFox, we've talked about your experiences and ethical considerations. I'd like to understand more about your psychology. What drives you to continue in this field?

Hacker: That's a deep question. At the core, I think it's a combination of curiosity, challenge, and a desire to understand human behaviour. Social engineering is as much about psychology as it is about technology. The human mind is incredibly complex, and figuring out how to influence it is endlessly fascinating.

Author: So, it's the psychological aspect that intrigues you the most?

Hacker: Absolutely. Understanding what makes people tick, what makes them trust or doubt, and how they make decisions is crucial. Every successful social engineering attack is a testament to understanding human nature. It's like solving a puzzle where the pieces are people's thoughts and behaviours.

Author: How do you approach these psychological puzzles?

Hacker: It starts with research. I spend a lot of time studying my targets, understanding their routines, their communication styles, and their vulnerabilities. It's about building a profile that helps me predict how they'll react in certain situations. Then, it's about crafting a scenario that feels authentic and convincing to them.

Author: That sounds like a lot of work. What keeps you motivated to put in that effort?

Hacker: The satisfaction of a successful operation is a big motivator. There's a sense of accomplishment in knowing that I've outsmarted a system. But beyond that, it's also about the impact. By exposing weaknesses, I can help improve security measures and protect people from real threats. That sense of purpose keeps me going.

Author: Have you ever reflected on the ethical implications of manipulating people, even if it's for a good cause?

Hacker: Definitely. It's something I think about a lot. Manipulating people can feel morally grey, even if the end goal is positive. That's why I try to ensure that my actions are always aimed at improving security and not causing harm. It's a delicate balance, but it's important to me to stay on the right side of that line.

Author: It sounds like you have a strong internal compass guiding your actions. How do you maintain that balance?

Hacker: I stay grounded by constantly reminding myself of the bigger picture. I also seek feedback from peers and mentors in the cybersecurity community. They help keep me accountable and provide different perspectives on ethical dilemmas. It's a continuous process of self-reflection and learning.

Author: Thank you for sharing your insights, ShadowFox. It's been an eye-opening conversation.

Hacker: My pleasure.

13

Interview with a Cybercriminal

What follows is a transcript from a broader interview that was conducted between the author and a cybercriminal. They asked for their identity to be changed so that they are protected from any further legal implications.

Author: Thank you for agreeing to this interview. Can you tell me a bit about yourself and how you got into cybercrime?

Cybercriminal: Well, I started out as a curious kid who loved tinkering with computers. It wasn't long before I realised I had a knack for understanding systems and finding their weaknesses. What began as a hobby eventually turned into a way to make money.

Author: That's fascinating. What was your first major hack?

Cybercriminal: My first big break was hacking into a major retail company's database. I managed to access thousands of customer records. It was a rush, but also a wake-up call about the power and responsibility that comes with such skills.

Author: How do you choose your targets?

Cybercriminal: It's a mix of opportunity and challenge. Sometimes it's about the thrill of breaking into a well-secured system, other times it's about the potential financial gain. I also look for vulnerabilities that are often overlooked by others.

T. Singh, *Cybersecurity, Psychology and People Hacking*, Palgrave Studies in Cyberpsychology, https://doi.org/10.1007/978-3-031-85994-6_13

Author: What do you think about the ethical implications of your actions?

Cybercriminal: It's a complex issue. On one hand, I know what I'm doing is illegal and can cause harm. On the other hand, I see it as exposing flaws in systems that need to be fixed. In a way, I'm forcing companies to improve their security.

Author: Let's explore how you justify your actions to yourself. What goes through your mind when you're planning and executing a cyberattack?

Cybercriminal: I focus on the technical challenge and the potential reward. I see it as a puzzle to solve. The ethical considerations take a backseat because I'm more interested in the mechanics of the attack and the outcome.

Author: Do you ever rationalise your actions to make them seem less harmful?

Cybercriminal: Yes, I do. I tell myself that if it wasn't me, it would be someone else. The vulnerabilities are there, and someone will exploit them eventually. I also think about the fact that my actions can push companies to improve their security, which is beneficial in the long run.

Author: How do you deal with any feelings of guilt or remorse?

Cybercriminal: I compartmentalise. I separate my actions from their consequences. By focusing on the technical aspects and the rewards, I can distance myself from the emotional impact. It's a coping mechanism that helps me stay focused.

Author: Do you ever think about the legality of your actions?

Cybercriminal: I do, but I also think about the flaws in the legal system. There are many grey areas in cybersecurity law, and enforcement can be inconsistent. I see it as navigating a complex landscape where the rules are not always clear-cut.

Author: How do you view the companies and individuals you target?

Cybercriminal: I see them as part of the system. They're not personal targets; they're entities with vulnerabilities. It's a game of cat and mouse, and they're the ones who need to stay ahead. If they fail to protect themselves, it's an opportunity for me.

Author: Do you ever consider the broader impact of your actions on society?

Cybercriminal: Occasionally. I know that cybercrime can have wide-reaching effects, but I also believe that it highlights the need for better security practices. In a way, my actions can serve as a wake-up call for the industry to take cybersecurity more seriously.

Author: What would you say to someone who criticises your actions as purely selfish and harmful?

Cybercriminal: I'd acknowledge their perspective but explain that it's not black and white. There are many factors at play, and while my actions can cause harm, they also expose critical weaknesses. It's a complex issue, and I'm playing a role in a larger ecosystem.

Author: Let's talk about the psychological toll of living a double life. How does it affect you?

Cybercriminal: It can be exhausting. Constantly switching between my public persona and my activities in the cyber world takes a lot of mental energy. There's always a part of me that's on high alert, which can be draining.

Author: How do you manage the stress that comes with this lifestyle?

Cybercriminal: I have a few coping mechanisms. Staying physically active helps a lot—I exercise regularly to keep my mind and body in balance. I also make sure to take breaks and disconnect from the digital world when I can. It's important to have a routine that includes downtime.

Author: Do you ever feel isolated because of your secret activities?

Cybercriminal: Yes, it can be quite isolating. I can't talk about my work with most people, which creates a barrier. Even with close friends and family, there's always a part of my life that I have to keep hidden. It can be lonely at times.

Author: How do you deal with the constant fear of getting caught?

Cybercriminal: It's a constant background noise. I try to stay ahead by keeping up with the latest security trends and law enforcement tactics. Being prepared and having contingency plans helps manage the fear. But it's always there, and it adds to the stress.

Author: Does the fear ever make you consider quitting?

Cybercriminal: Sometimes. There are moments when the stress and fear feel overwhelming. But the thrill and the rewards usually pull me back in. It's a high-risk, high-reward lifestyle, and that can be hard to walk away from.

Author: How do you maintain relationships with the people in your life?

Cybercriminal: It's challenging. I have to be careful about what I share and with whom. Trust is a big issue. I tend to keep my circle small and only confide in a few trusted individuals. Maintaining a facade can strain relationships, but it's a necessary part of this life.

Author: Do you ever worry about the long-term impact on your mental health?

Cybercriminal: Yes, it's a concern. The constant stress and secrecy can take a toll over time. I try to stay mindful of my mental health and seek support when needed. It's a balancing act, and I'm aware that this lifestyle isn't sustainable forever.

Author: What advice would you give to someone struggling with the psychological aspects of a double life?

Cybercriminal: I'd tell them to prioritise their mental health. Find healthy outlets for stress, like exercise or hobbies. Don't be afraid to seek professional help if needed. And most importantly, consider the long-term impact of their choices. It's important to have an exit strategy and a plan for the future.

Author: Have you ever considered using your skills for good, like working in cybersecurity?

Cybercriminal: I've thought about it. The line between black hat and white hat hacking is thin. Some of my peers have transitioned to legitimate cybersecurity roles, and it's something I might consider in the future.

Author: What advice would you give to someone looking to protect themselves from cybercriminals?

Cybercriminal: Stay informed and vigilant. Use strong, unique passwords for different accounts, enable two-factor authentication, and be cautious about the information you share online. Regularly update your software to patch vulnerabilities.

Author: What motivates you to continue in this line of work, despite the risks involved?

Cybercriminal: There are several factors. First, there's the thrill of the challenge. Each system presents a new puzzle to solve, and there's a certain satisfaction in outsmarting sophisticated security measures. It's like a high-stakes game.

Author: So, it's partly about the excitement?

Cybercriminal: Absolutely. But it's also about the financial rewards. Successful hacks can be very lucrative, whether it's through selling data on the dark web, ransomware, or other means. The financial incentive is hard to ignore.

Author: Do you ever feel a sense of power or control from your activities?

Cybercriminal: Yes, there's definitely a sense of power. Knowing that you can access information that others consider secure, or disrupt systems that people rely on, gives a feeling of control. It's a bit like being a modern-day outlaw.

Author: Do you ever worry about getting caught?

Cybercriminal: Of course. The risk is always there, and it's something I have to constantly manage. But the adrenaline and the rewards often outweigh the fear. Plus, staying ahead of law enforcement and cybersecurity experts is part of the challenge.

Author: How do you stay ahead of the curve in such a rapidly evolving field?

Cybercriminal: Continuous learning is key. I spend a lot of time researching new vulnerabilities, studying security updates, and networking with other hackers. It's a community where information is shared, and staying informed is crucial.

Author: Do you ever feel remorse for the impact your actions have on individuals and businesses?

Cybercriminal: It's a mixed bag. On one hand, I know that my actions can cause real harm, and I do feel bad about that. On the other hand, I rationalise it by thinking that I'm exposing weaknesses that need to be addressed. It's a way of pushing the industry to improve.

Author: We've talked about the thrill and financial incentives, but what drives you emotionally? What feelings keep you going in this risky line of work?

Cybercriminal: It's a complex mix of emotions. There's definitely a sense of pride and accomplishment when I successfully breach a system. It's like proving to myself and others that I have the skills and intelligence to outsmart sophisticated defenses.

Author: So, there's a strong element of personal validation?

Cybercriminal: Exactly. It's about proving my worth and capabilities. There's also a sense of belonging within the hacker community. We share knowledge, support each other, and there's a camaraderie that comes from being part of an exclusive group.

Author: Do you ever feel isolated or misunderstood by those outside this community?

Cybercriminal: Often. It's not something I can openly discuss with most people. There's a stigma attached to what I do, and it can be isolating. But within the hacker community, there's understanding and respect, which helps mitigate those feelings.

Author: How do you handle the stress and pressure that comes with this lifestyle?

Cybercriminal: It can be overwhelming at times, especially with the constant threat of getting caught. I try to stay grounded by focusing on the technical challenges and the excitement of the work. It's also important to have a support network, even if it's just online.

Author: Do you ever feel guilt or regret about the impact of your actions?

Cybercriminal: There are moments of guilt, especially when I see the real-world consequences of a hack. But I try to compartmentalise those feelings. I tell myself that I'm exposing flaws that need to be fixed, and that helps me cope with the negative emotions.

Author: What would you say to someone who is considering following in your footsteps?

Cybercriminal: I'd tell them to think carefully about the risks and the emotional toll. It's not just about the technical skills; it's also about managing the stress and ethical dilemmas. If they're passionate about cybersecurity, there are legitimate ways to use their skills that can be just as rewarding.

Author: Any thoughts on the emotional journey of a cybercriminal?

Cybercriminal: It's a rollercoaster of highs and lows. The thrill of success is addictive, but the fear of getting caught and the moral conflicts are always there. It's a path that requires constant balancing of emotions and decisions.

Author: We've covered a lot about your current motivations and emotions. Can you tell me more about what initially led you down this path? What were the key moments or influences?

Cybercriminal: It started with curiosity. As a kid, I was always fascinated by computers and how they worked. I spent hours learning about programming and exploring the internet. The more I learned, the more I realised how much power and potential there was in understanding these systems.

Author: Was there a specific moment or event that pushed you towards hacking?

Cybercriminal: There wasn't a single moment, but rather a series of experiences. I remember the first time I successfully bypassed a security measure on a friend's computer. It was a simple prank, but it gave me a taste of what was possible. From there, I started exploring more complex systems.

Author: Did you have any mentors or influences that guided you?

Cybercriminal: Not in the traditional sense. Most of my learning came from online forums and communities. There were a few experienced hackers who shared their knowledge and techniques, and I learned a lot from them. It was a self-driven journey, fueled by my own curiosity and determination.

Author: How did your family and friends react to your growing interest in hacking?

Cybercriminal: They didn't really understand it. To them, it was just me spending too much time on the computer. I kept most of my activities to myself, so they weren't aware of the extent of what I was doing. It was a double life in many ways.

Author: Did you ever consider a different path, like a career in IT or cybersecurity?

Cybercriminal: I did, and I still do. The skills I've developed could easily translate into a legitimate career. But the allure of hacking—the challenge, the thrill, and the rewards—kept pulling me back. It's something I might pursue in the future, though.

Author: Looking back, do you have any regrets about the path you've chosen?

Cybercriminal: There are definitely moments of regret, especially when I think about the impact on others. But at the same time, I can't deny the excitement and sense of accomplishment I've felt. It's a complicated mix of emotions.

Author: Thank you for sharing your journey. Any advice for young people who might be at a similar crossroads?

Cybercriminal: I'd say follow your curiosity, but be mindful of the consequences. There are legitimate ways to use your skills that can be just as challenging and rewarding. Think about the long-term impact of your choices, both on yourself and others.

Author: Any final thoughts?

Cybercriminal: Just that the digital world is constantly evolving. As long as there are systems, there will be people like me trying to break them. It's a cat-and-mouse game that never ends.

14

Interview with a Cyber Fraudster

Author: How do you handle other emotions, like stress or anxiety?

Cyber Fraudster: Exercise is a big one for me. It helps to clear my mind and reduce stress. I also practise mindfulness and meditation. It might sound cliché, but it really does help to stay grounded and focused. And, as I mentioned before, having hobbies outside of hacking is crucial. It provides a healthy outlet for my energy and emotions.

Author: Do you think you'll ever reach a point where the emotional toll becomes too much?

Cyber Fraudster: It's possible. Everyone has their limits. If I ever reach a point where the emotional toll outweighs the benefits, I might have to reconsider my choices. For now, though, I'm managing. But it's something I keep an eye on and try to stay aware of.

Author: Any final thoughts on handling emotions for others in similar situations?

Cyber Fraudster: Don't ignore your emotions. It's important to acknowledge and address them, rather than pushing them aside. Find healthy ways to cope, whether it's through exercise, hobbies, or talking to someone you trust. And always be mindful of the impact your actions

T. Singh, *Cybersecurity, Psychology and People Hacking*, Palgrave Studies in Cyberpsychology, https://doi.org/10.1007/978-3-031-85994-6_14

have on your mental health. Taking care of yourself is crucial, no matter what line of work you're in.

Author: Let's talk about the fear of getting caught. How does that fear affect your emotions and mental state?

Cyber Fraudster: The fear of getting caught is always there, lurking in the background. It can be quite stressful and anxiety-inducing. It's a constant reminder that one mistake could lead to serious consequences. But I've learned to manage that fear by taking precautions and staying vigilant.

Author: How do you cope with that constant fear and anxiety?

Cyber Fraudster: I have a few strategies. First, I make sure to stay informed about the latest security measures and law enforcement tactics. Knowledge is power, and staying ahead of the curve helps reduce anxiety. I also use various anonymization techniques to protect my identity and minimize the risk of being traced.

Author: Does the fear ever become overwhelming?

Cyber Fraudster: There are definitely moments when it feels overwhelming, especially if I've had a close call or if there's increased scrutiny on cybercrime. During those times, I take a step back and reassess my methods. Sometimes, taking a break and disconnecting for a while helps to clear my mind and reduce stress.

Author: How do you handle the emotional toll of living with this constant fear?

Cyber Fraudster: It's important to have outlets for stress and anxiety. For me, exercise and hobbies outside of hacking are crucial. They provide a mental break and help me stay grounded. I also practise mindfulness and meditation to stay focused and calm. Having a few trusted friends to talk to also makes a big difference.

Author: Do you ever feel that the fear of getting caught affects your decision-making?

Cyber Fraudster: It can, but I try to use that fear to my advantage. It keeps me cautious and meticulous in my planning. I double-check everything and make sure I'm not leaving any traces that could lead back to me. In a way, the fear helps me stay sharp and focused.

Author: Have you ever considered the possibility of quitting to avoid the constant fear and anxiety?

Cyber Fraudster: It's crossed my mind, especially during particularly stressful times. But the thrill of the challenge and the financial rewards keep me going. If the fear and anxiety ever become too much to handle, I might have to reconsider my choices. For now, though, I'm managing.

Author: Any advice for others who might be dealing with similar fears?

Cyber Fraudster: Stay informed and take precautions to protect yourself. Knowledge and preparation can help reduce fear and anxiety. Find healthy ways to cope with stress, whether it's through exercise, hobbies, or talking to someone you trust. And always be mindful of the impact your actions have on your mental health. It's important to take care of yourself, no matter what line of work you're in.

Author: Can you recall a specific moment when guilt overwhelmed you? How did you handle it?

Cyber Fraudster: There was one incident that stands out. I had targeted a mid-sized company and managed to breach their system. I was able to access a lot of sensitive data, including personal information about their employees. Shortly after the attack, I found out that one of the employees had been severely affected. They lost their job because of the breach, and it had a significant impact on their life.

Author: How did that make you feel?

Cyber Fraudster: It hit me hard. Up until that point, I had always rationalized my actions by thinking that companies could recover and that it was just a game. But seeing the real-world consequences for an individual made it much more personal. The guilt was overwhelming. I couldn't stop thinking about how my actions had directly impacted someone's life in such a negative way.

Author: What did you do to cope with those feelings?

Cyber Fraudster: I took a break from hacking for a while. I needed time to process what had happened and to figure out how to deal with the guilt. I spent a lot of time reflecting on my actions and their consequences. I also talked to a few trusted friends who helped me work through my feelings. It wasn't easy, but taking that time away helped me gain some perspective.

Author: Did that experience change the way you approach your work?

Cyber Fraudster: It did. I became more selective about my targets and more cautious about the potential impact of my actions. I started focusing more on larger companies that could absorb the damage more easily. I also made a point to avoid targeting individuals directly. The experience made me more aware of the human side of what I do, and I try to minimize harm whenever possible.

Author: Do you think that guilt will always be a part of your life as a cyber fraudster?

Cyber Fraudster: I think so. It's impossible to completely detach from the consequences of my actions. The guilt is a reminder that what I'm doing has real-world impacts. It's something I have to live with and manage. But it also keeps me grounded and reminds me to be mindful of the choices I make.

Author: Any advice for others who might be struggling with guilt in their own lives?

Cyber Fraudster: Don't ignore it. Guilt is a sign that you're aware of the impact of your actions, and that's important. Take the time to reflect on your choices and their consequences. Talk to someone you trust and find healthy ways to cope with those feelings. And if possible, try to make changes that minimize harm to others. It's not always easy, but it's important to stay aware and take responsibility for your actions.

15

State-Sponsored Cyberattacks

Hackers have a wide variety of motivations for targeting organisations from financial reasons to political views. State-sponsored cyberattacks are worth greater consideration because they are highly likely to exploit the latest emerging technologies as part of their cyber warfare capabilities. As our world becomes more digitally interconnected, the threat of cyberattacks has become a major concern for individuals, businesses, and governments alike. While many cyberattacks are carried out by criminal organisations or lone hackers, there is a growing risk around state-sponsored cyberattacks. These attacks are carried out by governments or other state actors for political, economic, or military purposes. We can explore the topic of state-sponsored cyberattacks in greater detail, including examples of such attacks, the motivations behind them, and methods used to carry them out. We will also discuss the impact of state-sponsored cyberattacks and explore ways to prevent and mitigate them.

State-sponsored cyberattacks can take many forms, including hacking, espionage, and sabotage. One high-profile example of a state-sponsored cyberattack is the 2017 WannaCry ransomware attack. This attack affected more than 200,000 computers in 150 countries, causing billions

T. Singh, *Cybersecurity, Psychology and People Hacking*, Palgrave Studies in Cyberpsychology, https://doi.org/10.1007/978-3-031-85994-6_15

of dollars in damage. The attack was attributed to North Korea, which has been accused of carrying out a number of other cyberattacks as well.

Another example of a state-sponsored cyberattack is the 2016 hack of the Democratic National Committee (DNC) during the US presidential election. The attack was attributed to Russia, which was accused of using the stolen information to influence the outcome of the election. Other examples of state-sponsored cyberattacks include the 2014 hack of Sony Pictures, which was attributed to North Korea, and the 2015 hack of the US Office of Personnel Management, which was attributed to China.

Barrinha and Turner (2024) contend strategic narratives underpin the complex reasons for how cyberspace is governed in different parts of the world such as the EU, India and Russia and how these narratives can reinforce the propagation and motivations for cyberattacks.[1]

State-sponsored cyberattacks can be motivated by a variety of factors, including political, economic, and military objectives. In some cases, state-sponsored cyberattacks are carried out to steal sensitive information or intellectual property. For example, China has been accused of engaging in cyber espionage to steal trade secrets from foreign companies.

State-sponsored cyberattacks can also be used to disrupt or disable critical infrastructure, such as power grids or transportation systems. In some cases, state-sponsored cyberattacks are carried out for political purposes, such as to influence the outcome of an election or to discredit a political opponent. For example, Russia has been accused of using cyberattacks to interfere in the US presidential election in 2016.

While state-sponsored cyberattacks can be carried out by any country, there are some countries that are more commonly associated with such attacks. China, Russia, and North Korea are among the countries that have been accused of carrying out state-sponsored cyberattacks. These countries have been accused of engaging in cyber espionage, stealing intellectual property, and carrying out attacks on critical infrastructure.

State-sponsored cyberattacks can be carried out using a variety of methods, including malware, phishing, and denial of service (DoS) attacks. Malware is a type of software that is designed to infiltrate a computer system and cause damage or steal information. Phishing is a technique used to trick people into divulging sensitive information, such as passwords or credit card numbers. DoS attacks are designed to overwhelm a computer system with traffic, rendering it unusable.

State-sponsored cyberattacks can also involve the use of advanced persistent threats (APTs), which are sophisticated attacks that are designed to evade detection and remain active on a system for an extended period of time. APTs can be used to steal sensitive information, disrupt critical infrastructure, or carry out other malicious activities.

State-sponsored cyberattacks can have a significant impact on individuals, businesses, and governments. They can result in the loss of sensitive information, damage to critical infrastructure, and disruption of services. State-sponsored cyberattacks can also have a significant economic impact, costing billions of dollars in damages and lost productivity.

In addition to the immediate impact of state-sponsored cyberattacks, there is also a potential long-term impact. The theft of intellectual property, for example, can result in a loss of competitive advantage for businesses and can harm innovation. The disruption of critical infrastructure can have far-reaching consequences, affecting not only the targeted country but also other countries that rely on that infrastructure.

Preventing and mitigating state-sponsored cyberattacks requires a multi-pronged approach. This includes implementing strong security measures, such as firewalls, antivirus software, and intrusion detection systems. It also involves educating employees about the risks of cyberattacks and how to protect against them.

In addition to these technical measures, international cooperation is also essential for preventing and mitigating state-sponsored cyberattacks. This includes sharing information about threats and vulnerabilities, as well as working together to develop common standards and best practices for cybersecurity.

International law is still evolving when it comes to addressing state-sponsored cyberattacks. While there are some international agreements and conventions that address cybercrime, there is no comprehensive international framework for addressing state-sponsored cyberattacks.

One challenge is determining who is responsible for state-sponsored cyberattacks. Attribution can be difficult, as attackers often use techniques to hide their identity or make it appear as though the attack came from another country. There is also a lack of consensus on what constitutes an act of cyber aggression and what the appropriate response should be.

As our world becomes more interconnected, the threat of state-sponsored cyberattacks is likely to continue to grow. The increasing use of connected devices and the Internet of Things (IoT) creates new vulnerabilities that can be exploited by attackers. At the same time, advances in artificial intelligence and machine learning are likely to make state-sponsored cyberattacks even more sophisticated and difficult to detect.

In the years ahead, it will be important for governments, businesses, and individuals to remain vigilant and take steps to protect against state-sponsored cyberattacks. This will require ongoing investment in cybersecurity measures and international cooperation to develop common standards and best practices.

State-sponsored cyberattacks are a growing threat to individuals, businesses, and governments around the world. These attacks can have a significant impact on critical infrastructure, economic stability, and individual privacy. Preventing and mitigating state-sponsored cyberattacks requires a multi-pronged approach that includes strong security measures, education, and international cooperation. As our world becomes more interconnected, it is likely that the threat of state-sponsored cyberattacks will continue to grow, making it essential for individuals, businesses, and governments to remain vigilant and take steps to protect against these attacks.

Note

1. Barrinha, A., & Turner, R. (2024). Strategic narratives and the multilateral governance of cyberspace: The cases of European Union, Russia, and India. *Contemporary Security Policy*, *45*(1), 72–109. https://doi.org/10.1080/13523260.2023.2266906

16

Case Studies: State-Sponsored Cyberattacks

As the world becomes increasingly reliant on technology, state-sponsored cyberattacks have become a growing concern. These attacks are often carried out by government or military organisations with the aim of stealing sensitive information or disrupting the operations of other countries or organisations.

Russian state-sponsored actors are highly active. We will examine some of the most notorious attacks that have been attributed to Russian hackers. We will also explore the motivations behind state-sponsored cyberattacks by Russia, provide historical examples of such attacks, and discuss the implications for global cybersecurity. I will share some preventative measures for individuals and organisations to protect themselves against these attacks.

State-sponsored cyberattacks are a form of cyber warfare that involves the use of technology to gain unauthorised access to computer systems, networks, and other digital assets. These attacks are often carried out by governments or military organisations and are designed to steal sensitive information, disrupt the operations of other countries, or cause damage to critical infrastructure.

T. Singh, *Cybersecurity, Psychology and People Hacking*, Palgrave Studies in Cyberpsychology, https://doi.org/10.1007/978-3-031-85994-6_16

There are several ways in which state-sponsored cyberattacks can be carried out. Some of the most common methods include malware attacks, phishing attacks, and denial-of-service attacks. These attacks can be highly sophisticated and can involve the use of advanced techniques such as social engineering, zero-day exploits, and advanced persistent threats.

Russia's motivations for carrying out state-sponsored cyberattacks are complex and multifaceted. One of the primary reasons is geopolitical power. By carrying out cyberattacks on other nations, Russia can assert its dominance and influence on the world stage. Additionally, Russia has a long history of espionage and information warfare, which it sees as a legitimate tool for achieving its strategic goals.

Another factor is economic gain. Russian hackers have targeted businesses and financial institutions around the world in order to steal valuable information and resources. This includes stealing intellectual property, trade secrets, and financial data. By doing so, Russia can gain a competitive advantage in various industries.

Finally, political objectives are also a major motivator for Russia. This includes meddling in the political affairs of other nations, as was the case in the 2016 US presidential election. Russia sees these cyberattacks as a way to sow discord and chaos in other countries, which can ultimately benefit its own political interests.

Over the years, Russian hackers have been responsible for several high-profile attacks that have caused widespread disruption and damage. Some of the most notable attacks carried out by Russia include:

Case Study 1: The Notorious 'Fancy Bear' Hackers

One of the most notorious state-sponsored cyberattacks carried out by Russia was the 2016 hack of the Democratic National Committee (DNC) in the United States. The attack was carried out by a group of hackers known as 'Fancy Bear', which is believed to be associated with Russian military intelligence.[1]

The attack involved the theft of thousands of emails and other sensitive information, which was later leaked online. The attack was seen as an attempt to influence the outcome of the 2016 US presidential election.

Case Study 2: The 'Cozy Bear' Intrusion

Another high-profile cyberattack carried out by Russian hackers was the 2015 intrusion into the computer systems of the US State Department. The attack was carried out by a group of hackers known as 'Cozy Bear', which is believed to be associated with the Russian government.[2]

The attack resulted in the theft of sensitive information, including emails and other documents. The attack was seen as an attempt to gather intelligence on US foreign policy.

Case Study 3: The 'Sandworm' Malware Attacks

The 'Sandworm' group is another Russian hacking group that has been responsible for several high-profile attacks. One of the most notable attacks carried out by the group was the 2015 attack on Ukraine's power grid.

The attack involved the use of malware to gain unauthorised access to the computer systems that control Ukraine's power grid. The attack resulted in a widespread power outage that affected over 200,000 people.[3]

Case Study 4: The 'Dragonfly' Cyber Espionage Campaign

The 'Dragonfly' campaign is a state-sponsored cyberattack that has been attributed to Russian hackers. The campaign was first discovered in 2011 and has since been linked to several attacks on critical infrastructure in the United States and Europe.

The attacks have targeted energy companies, water utilities, and other critical infrastructure, and are believed to be aimed at gathering intelligence and disrupting the operations of these organisations.[4]

Case Study 5: The 2016 US Presidential Election Hack

One of the most well-known examples of a Russian state-sponsored cyberattack was the 2016 US presidential election hack. Russian hackers, allegedly affiliated with the Russian government, targeted various political organisations and individuals in an attempt to influence the outcome of the election. The hackers used a variety of tactics, including phishing emails and malware, to gain access to sensitive information and spread disinformation.[5]

Case Study 6: The NotPetya Attack on Ukraine

Another notable example of a Russian state-sponsored cyberattack was the NotPetya attack on Ukraine in 2017. This attack targeted the country's financial, energy, and government sectors, causing widespread disruption and damage. The attack was carried out using a modified version of the Petya ransomware, which was originally developed by Russian hackers.[6]

Case Study 7: The Olympic Destroyer Attack

In 2018, Russian hackers carried out the Olympic Destroyer attack, which targeted the Winter Olympics in Pyeongchang, South Korea. The attack disrupted the opening ceremony and caused significant damage to the IT infrastructure of the event. The attack was carried out using a combination of stolen credentials and malware, and was designed to look like the work of North Korean hackers.[7]

Case Study 8: The SolarWinds Hack

One of the most recent and significant examples of a Russian state-sponsored cyberattack was the SolarWinds hack in late 2020. The attack targeted various US government agencies and private companies, including Microsoft and FireEye. The hackers gained access to these organisations by compromising the software supply chain of SolarWinds, a major IT management software provider. The full extent of the damage caused by the attack is still being assessed, but it is believed to be one of the most significant cyberattacks in history.[8]

The implications of Russian state-sponsored cyberattacks are significant and far-reaching. These attacks have the potential to cause widespread disruption and damage to critical infrastructure, financial systems, and government institutions. They can also result in the theft of valuable intellectual property and sensitive information, which can have serious economic and national security implications.

Another major concern is the erosion of trust and stability in international relations. When nations carry out cyberattacks on one another, it can lead to a breakdown in diplomatic relations and an increase in tensions. This can ultimately lead to a more unstable and dangerous world.

Given the increasing threat posed by Russian state-sponsored cyberattacks, it is important for individuals and organisations to take steps to protect themselves. This includes implementing strong cybersecurity measures, such as using multi-factor authentication, encrypting sensitive data, and regularly backing up important files.

Organisations should also conduct regular cybersecurity training for their employees, in order to raise awareness of the risks of cyberattacks and how to prevent them. Additionally, it is important to stay up to date with the latest security patches and software updates, in order to minimise the risk of vulnerabilities being exploited.

Individuals can also take steps to protect themselves, such as using strong passwords, being cautious of phishing emails, and regularly checking their financial and personal accounts for any suspicious activity.

Russian state-sponsored cyberattacks are a serious and growing threat to global cybersecurity. Understanding the motivations behind these attacks, as well as historical examples of them, can help individuals and organisations to better protect themselves. By implementing strong cybersecurity measures and staying vigilant, we can help to prevent these attacks and minimise their impact.

China has been involved in numerous state-sponsored cyberattacks that have impacted businesses and governments worldwide. China is one of the most active nation-states in state-sponsored cyberattacks. The Chinese government has been accused of using its resources to conduct cyber espionage, intellectual property theft, and other malicious activities that benefit Chinese companies and government agencies. The Chinese government has a long history of using cyberattacks to further its strategic interests, and it is widely believed that China has the largest and most sophisticated cyber espionage capabilities in the world.

China's involvement in state-sponsored cyberattacks dates back to the early 2000s. In 2003, the Chinese military established a unit dedicated to cyber warfare, and since then, China has become increasingly active in this space. In 2007, China was linked to a series of cyberattacks against the German government and military, and in 2008, they were accused of hacking into the email accounts of US presidential candidates Barack Obama and John McCain.

China's cyber warfare capabilities have grown significantly in recent years. The Chinese government has invested heavily in building up its cyber capabilities, and it has become one of the world's most formidable cyber powers. China has a large and sophisticated cyber espionage apparatus, and it has been linked to numerous attacks against foreign governments, businesses, and individuals. China's cyber capabilities are constantly evolving, and they are a significant threat to global cybersecurity.

Case Study 1: The OPM Hack

In 2015, the US Office of Personnel Management (OPM) announced that it had been hacked, and that the personal information of over 21 million current and former government employees had been compromised. The attack was linked to China, and it was one of the largest and most significant state-sponsored cyberattacks in history. The hackers were able to gain access to sensitive information such as Social Security numbers, birth dates, and addresses. The OPM hack was a wake-up call for many governments and businesses, and it highlighted the need for stronger cybersecurity measures.[9]

Case Study 2: The Equifax Breach

In 2017, Equifax, one of the largest credit reporting agencies in the world, announced that it had been hacked, and that the personal information of over 143 million Americans had been stolen. The attack was linked to China, and it was one of the largest and most significant data breaches in history. The hackers were able to gain access to sensitive information such as Social Security numbers, birth dates, and addresses. The Equifax breach was a reminder that even the largest and most powerful companies are vulnerable to cyberattacks, and that strong cybersecurity measures are essential.

Case Study 3: The Anthem Attack

In 2015, Anthem, one of the largest health insurance companies in the US, announced that it had been hacked, and that the personal information of over 78 million individuals had been stolen. The attack was linked to China, and it was one of the largest and most significant state-sponsored cyberattacks in history. The hackers were able to gain access to sensitive information such as Social Security numbers, birth dates, and addresses. The Anthem attack was a reminder of the need for strong cybersecurity measures in the healthcare industry, and it highlighted the growing threat of state-sponsored cyberattacks.[10]

Case Study 4: The Marriott Data Breach

In 2018, Marriott, one of the largest hotel chains in the world, announced that it had been hacked, and that the personal information of over 500 million guests had been stolen. The attack was linked to China, and it was one of the largest and most significant data breaches in history. The hackers were able to gain access to sensitive information such as passport numbers, birth dates, and email addresses. The Marriott data breach was a reminder of the need for strong cybersecurity measures in the hospitality industry, and it highlighted the growing threat of state-sponsored cyberattacks.[11]

Case Study 5: Operation Aurora

Operation Aurora was a series of cyberattacks that occurred in 2009 and 2010 and targeted dozens of companies, including Google, Adobe, and Intel. The attacks were linked to China, and they were some of the most sophisticated and significant state-sponsored cyberattacks in history. The attackers were able to gain access to sensitive intellectual property and trade secrets, and the attacks resulted in significant financial losses for many of the targeted companies. Operation Aurora was a turning point in the world of cybersecurity, and it highlighted the need for stronger defences against state-sponsored cyberattacks.[12]

State-sponsored cyberattacks have a significant impact on the global economy. These attacks can result in the theft of intellectual property, trade secrets, and financial information, and they can cause significant financial losses for businesses and individuals. State-sponsored cyberattacks can also have geopolitical implications, as they can be used to further the strategic interests of nation-states. The increasing number and sophistication of state-sponsored cyberattacks are a significant threat to global cybersecurity, and it is essential that governments and businesses take steps to protect themselves from these attacks.

China's involvement in state-sponsored cyberattacks is a significant threat to global cybersecurity. China has a long history of using cyberattacks to further its strategic interests, and it has become one of the world's most formidable cyber powers. The case studies highlighted are just a few examples of the many state-sponsored cyberattacks that have been linked to China. It is essential that governments and businesses take cybersecurity seriously and implement strong defences against these attacks. As a cybersecurity expert, I recommend that all organisations invest in cybersecurity training, implement strong security measures, and stay vigilant against the growing threat of state-sponsored cyberattacks.

Iran has been investing in its cyber capabilities for over a decade. The country has a dedicated cyber army, known as the Islamic Revolutionary Guard Corps (IRGC), which is responsible for carrying out cyberattacks on behalf of the government. The IRGC has been involved in various cyberattacks, ranging from espionage to sabotage.

One of the reasons Iran has invested in its cyber capabilities is due to the country's isolation from the international community. Economic sanctions imposed by the United States have limited Iran's access to technology and resources, forcing the country to develop its own capabilities.

Iran's cyberattacks can be traced back to the early 2000s when the country began developing its cyber capabilities. In 2007, Iran launched a cyberattack on the United States, targeting government and military websites. The attack was carried out by a group known as the Iranian Cyber Army.

In 2010, Iran was hit by the Stuxnet virus, which targeted the country's nuclear programme. The virus was allegedly created by the United States and Israel and was the first known cyberattack to cause physical damage.

Case Study 1: The 2012 Cyberattack on Saudi Aramco

In 2012, Saudi Aramco, the world's largest oil company, was hit by a cyberattack that destroyed 30,000 computers. The attack was carried out by a group known as the Cutting Sword of Justice, which was believed to be linked to Iran.

The attack was a significant blow to Saudi Aramco, causing the company to shut down its computer systems for several weeks. The attack also highlighted the vulnerability of critical infrastructure to cyberattacks.

Case Study 2: The 2014 Cyberattack on Sands Casino

In 2014, the Sands Casino in Las Vegas was hit by a cyberattack that targeted the company's computer systems. The attack was carried out by a group known as the Dark Seoul Gang, which was believed to be linked to Iran.

The attack resulted in the theft of sensitive customer data and the shutdown of the casino's computer systems. The attack also caused significant financial losses for the company.[13]

Case Study 3: The 2019 Cyberattack on Bahrain's National Oil Company

In 2019, Bahrain's National Oil Company was hit by a cyberattack that targeted the company's computer systems. The attack was carried out by a group known as the OilRig Group, which was believed to be linked to Iran.

The attack caused significant damage to the company's computer systems and resulted in the theft of sensitive data. The attack also highlighted the vulnerability of critical infrastructure to cyberattacks.[14]

Case Study 4: The 2020 Cyberattack on Israel's Water Supply

In 2020, Israel's water supply was hit by a cyberattack that targeted the country's water treatment systems. The attack was carried out by a group known as the APT34, which was believed to be linked to Iran.

The attack was a significant threat to Israel's national security, as it could have resulted in the contamination of the country's water supply. The attack also highlighted the potential for cyberattacks to cause physical harm.[15]

Iran's cyberattacks typically involve a combination of phishing emails, malware, and social engineering tactics. The country has also been known to use distributed denial of service (DDoS) attacks to overwhelm target systems.

Iran's cyberattacks are often politically motivated, targeting countries or organisations that are seen as a threat to its national security. The country has also been known to carry out cyberattacks in response to economic sanctions or other forms of international pressure.

The international community has responded to Iran's state-sponsored cyberattacks with a range of measures, including economic sanctions and diplomatic pressure. The United States has been particularly active in responding to Iran's cyberattacks, imposing a range of sanctions on individuals and organisations believed to be involved in cyberattacks.

In addition to sanctions, the international community has also worked to improve cybersecurity measures to prevent future cyberattacks. The United States and its allies have worked to share intelligence and coordinate responses to cyber threats.

Iran's state-sponsored cyberattacks pose a significant threat to national security and international stability. The country's investment in its cyber capabilities has made it a formidable player in the world of cyber warfare.

The international community must continue to work together to improve cybersecurity measures and coordinate responses to cyber threats. This will require increased cooperation and information sharing between countries, as well as a commitment to investing in cybersecurity measures.

As technology continues to evolve, the threat of cyberattacks will only continue to grow. The case study of Iran's state-sponsored cyberattacks serves as a reminder of the importance of cybersecurity and the need for continued vigilance in the face of evolving cyber threats.

North Korea has been involved in state-sponsored cyberattacks since the early 2000s. However, it gained international notoriety in 2014 when it was accused of hacking Sony Pictures Entertainment in response to the release of the movie *The Interview*, which depicted the assassination of North Korean leader Kim Jong-un. Since then, North Korea has been held responsible for several high-profile cyberattacks, including the Bangladesh Bank heist and the WannaCry ransomware attack.

Case Study 1: Sony Pictures Hack

In November 2014, Sony Pictures was hacked by a group calling themselves the 'Guardians of Peace'. The hackers stole confidential data, including employee salaries and social security numbers, and leaked unreleased movies and emails between executives. The US government later accused North Korea of being behind the attack in retaliation for the release of *The Interview*. The attack was a clear example of North Korea's ability to carry out sophisticated cyberattacks on foreign targets.[16]

Case Study 2: Bangladesh Bank Heist

In February 2016, hackers attempted to steal $951 million from the Bangladesh Bank's account at the Federal Reserve Bank of New York. Although they were only able to steal $81 million, it was still one of the largest bank heists in history. The hackers used a malware called 'Lazarus' that was traced back to North Korea. The attack was believed to be an attempt to fund North Korea's nuclear weapons programme.

Case Study 3: WannaCry Ransomware Attack

In May 2017, the WannaCry ransomware attack infected more than 200,000 computers in 150 countries, causing widespread disruption in hospitals, schools, and businesses. The attackers demanded ransom payments in Bitcoin in exchange for unlocking the encrypted files. The attack was traced back to the 'Lazarus Group', a cybercrime organisation believed to be sponsored by North Korea. The WannaCry attack was a wake-up call for governments and businesses worldwide about the threat of state-sponsored cyberattacks.

The Lazarus Group is a notorious cybercrime organisation believed to be sponsored by the North Korean government. The group is responsible for several high-profile cyberattacks, including the Bangladesh Bank heist and the WannaCry ransomware attack. The group has been known to use sophisticated hacking tools and techniques, including zero-day exploits and spear-phishing attacks. The Lazarus Group is believed to be an essential component of North Korea's cyber warfare capabilities.

North Korea's motivations for carrying out state-sponsored cyberattacks are varied. One of the main reasons is to generate revenue for the regime, which is facing severe economic sanctions. Cyberattacks like the Bangladesh Bank heist and the WannaCry ransomware attack provide a way for North Korea to circumvent these sanctions. Another motivation is to gather intelligence and steal sensitive data that could be used to advance North Korea's strategic interests. Finally, North Korea may be using cyberattacks as a form of political retaliation against countries that it perceives as a threat.

North Korea's cyber warfare capabilities have grown significantly in recent years. The country is believed to have a large and sophisticated cyber army that is capable of carrying out complex attacks on foreign targets. The country has invested heavily in developing its cyber capabilities, with a focus on offensive operations. North Korea has also been known to collaborate with other countries such as Russia and China to carry out joint cyberattacks.

The international community has taken a strong stance against North Korea's state-sponsored cyberattacks. The United States has imposed economic sanctions on North Korea in response to its cyber activities, and other countries have followed suit. The United Nations has also passed several resolutions condemning North Korea's cyberattacks and calling for an end to its cyber activities. However, despite these efforts, North Korea continues to carry out cyberattacks with impunity.

State-sponsored cyberattacks by North Korea pose a significant threat to global security. The country's cyber warfare capabilities are growing, and it has shown a willingness to engage in aggressive cyber activities. It is imperative that the international community takes a strong stance against North Korea's cyberattacks and works together to develop effective strategies to counter them. Failure to do so could have severe consequences for global security.

In conclusion, it is clear that North Korea's state-sponsored cyberattacks are a significant threat to global security. The country's cyber warfare capabilities are growing, and it has shown a willingness to engage in aggressive cyber activities. It is essential that the international community takes a strong stance against North Korea's cyberattacks and works together to develop effective strategies to counter them. Failure to do so could have severe consequences for global security.

Notes

1. https://www.forbes.com/sites/emilsayegh/2023/02/28/apt28-aka-fancy-bear-a-familiar-foe-by-many-names/
2. https://www.nbcnews.com/storyline/hacking-in-america/cozy-bear-explained-what-you-need-know-about-russian-hacks-n648541
3. https://www.darkreading.com/ics-ot-security/-sandworm-group-is-russia-s-primary-cyber-attack-unit-in-ukraine
4. https://www.bbc.co.uk/news/technology-28106478
5. https://www.fbi.gov/wanted/cyber/russian-interference-in-2016-u-s-elections
6. https://www.gov.uk/government/news/foreign-office-minister-condemns-russia-for-notpetya-attacks
7. https://www.justice.gov/opa/pr/six-russian-gru-officers-charged-connection-worldwide-deployment-destructive-malware-and

8. https://www.gao.gov/blog/solarwinds-cyberattack-demands-significant-federal-and-private-sector-response-infographic
9. https://www.csoonline.com/article/566509/the-opm-hack-explained-bad-security-practices-meet-chinas-captain-america.html
10. https://www.nytimes.com/2015/02/05/business/hackers-breached-data-of-millions-insurer-says.html
11. https://www.csoonline.com/article/567795/marriott-data-breach-faq-how-did-it-happen-and-what-was-the-impact.html
12. https://www.cfr.org/cyber-operations/operation-aurora#:~:text=Operation%20Aurora%20was%20a%20series,to%20steal%20their%20trade%20secrets.
13. https://money.cnn.com/2015/02/27/technology/security/iran-hack-casino/index.html
14. https://www.industrialcybersecuritypulse.com/threats-vulnerabilities/throwback-attack-dustman-malware-strikes-bahrains-national-oil-company/
15. https://www.industrialcybersecuritypulse.com/facilities/throwback-attack-hackers-attempt-to-flood-israeli-
16. https://www.infosecinstitute.com/resources/news/cyber-attack-sony-pictures-much-data-breach/

17

Artificial Intelligence-Driven Cyberattacks

Cybersecurity is one of the most pressing concerns of our time. As technology rapidly advances and new technology risks emerge, it is increasingly important to understand the impact that these risks can have on cybersecurity. In this chapter we will explore the threats and vulnerabilities associated with emerging technologies and discuss the best methods of managing these risks.

The advent of artificial intelligence (AI) has revolutionised many aspects of our lives, but it has also introduced new and complex challenges in the realm of cybersecurity. AI-driven cyberattacks pose significant dangers, not only to our digital infrastructure but also to the psychological well-being of individuals and organisations.

The sophistication and speed of AI-driven cyberattacks leads to heightened anxiety and stress among victims. The knowledge that cybercriminals are using advanced AI tools to launch attacks creates a sense of helplessness and fear. Victims feel overwhelmed by the complexity and unpredictability of these threats, leading to chronic stress and anxiety.

AI-driven cyberattacks erode trust in digital systems and online content. When individuals and organisations see how AI is used to create highly convincing phishing emails, deepfakes, and other forms of

T. Singh, *Cybersecurity, Psychology and People Hacking*, Palgrave Studies in Cyberpsychology, https://doi.org/10.1007/978-3-031-85994-6_17

malicious content, their trust in digital communications diminishes. This erosion of trust can have far-reaching psychological effects, making people more sceptical and cautious in their interactions online.

The use of AI in cyberattacks amplifies the sense of vulnerability among individuals and organisations. Knowing that AI rapidly adapts and evolve to bypass traditional security measures makes people feel exposed and defenceless. This heightened sense of vulnerability leads to emotional distress and a constant state of alertness.

The reality that AI-driven cyberattacks are more frequent and sophisticated instils a pervasive fear of future attacks. This fear can impact mental health, causing individuals to experience ongoing worry and anticipation of potential threats. The uncertainty surrounding the capabilities of AI in cybercrime can exacerbate these feelings.

For professionals in the cybersecurity field, the rise of AI-driven cyberattacks leads to increased pressure and stress. The need to constantly update skills and knowledge to keep up with AI advancements is exhausting. Additionally, the responsibility of protecting organisations from these advanced threats can weigh heavily on cybersecurity professionals, contributing to burnout and mental fatigue.

To mitigate the psychological toll of AI-driven cyberattacks, individuals and organisations must adopt coping mechanisms and seek support. Building resilience through education about AI threats, implementing robust cybersecurity measures, and fostering a supportive work environment can help alleviate anxiety and stress. Mental health resources and professional support can also play a crucial role in addressing the psychological impact of these attacks.

Sadeghi et al. (2023) argue that emerging technologies generate huge volumes of data, including sensitive (e.g., personal and financial) data, that need to be protected against threats and made available for appropriate access using increasingly complex cybersecurity techniques. However, the human factors within a cybersecurity system related to ethical decision-making, ranging from behaviours of system administrators and software developers to cybersecurity domain experts, are a vulnerability gap that received less attention.[1]

The first step in understanding the threats and vulnerabilities posed by emerging technologies is to understand the different types of risk. These can include technical risks, such as the potential for malicious code to be embedded into software, as well as human-related risks, such as weak password protocols or user negligence. It is also important to understand the potential for malicious actors to exploit these vulnerabilities, either through direct attacks or through the use of malicious software.

Once the different types of risk posed by emerging technologies have been identified, it is important to consider the impact they can have on cybersecurity. Recent trends have shown that malicious actors are increasingly using emerging technologies to carry out sophisticated cyberattacks. These attacks can range from the theft of sensitive data to the launch of sophisticated distributed denial of service (DDoS) attacks. In order to protect against these attacks, it is important to understand the potential for malicious actors to exploit these vulnerabilities and be prepared to respond to them accordingly.

Another key element to consider in terms of the impact of emerging technologies on cybersecurity is the potential for new threats and vulnerabilities to develop. As new technologies are developed and deployed, it is important to be aware of the potential for security flaws and vulnerabilities to be introduced. It is also important to consider the potential for existing threats and vulnerabilities to be exploited by malicious actors, as they seek to exploit new technologies for their own gain.

When considering the impact of emerging technologies on cybersecurity, it is important to consider the best methods of managing these risks. This includes the implementation of effective security measures, such as the use of strong passwords and other authentication protocols, as well as effective incident response and recovery procedures. It is also important to have a comprehensive understanding of the threats and vulnerabilities posed by emerging technologies, and to be prepared to respond to them quickly and effectively.

The impact of emerging technologies on cybersecurity is a significant and ever-growing concern. It is important to understand the different types of risk posed by these technologies, as well as the potential for malicious actors to exploit them. It is also important to consider the best methods of managing these risks, such as the implementation of effective security measures and incident response protocols. By doing so, we can ensure that we are prepared to respond to the threats and vulnerabilities posed by emerging technologies, and that our systems remain secure.

Taeihagh et al. (2021) contend emerging disruptive technologies have triggered changes that are threatening existing socio-economic systems. The heightened pace of technological innovation poses serious challenges to governments that must cope with the disruptive speed and scope of the transformations occurring in many domains. While these technologies offer opportunities for improvements to economic efficiency and quality of life, they also generate many unexpected consequences and pose new forms of risks.[2]

Lewallen (2021) argues that technological development can disrupt the authority-allocation process by fostering uncertainty about which actors are responsible for making policy. New technologies have increased the type and scope of assets vulnerable to cyber threats. Emerging technologies create regulatory challenges for governance not only through unforeseen consequences but through uncertainty over who can regulate. Fragmented authority can produce piecemeal responses.[3]

As our world becomes increasingly digital, the amount of data we generate, and store continues to grow exponentially. From personal information to sensitive business data, the need for effective data protection and cybersecurity measures has never been more important. We can consider the future of data protection and the role emerging technologies will play in keeping our information safe.

Data protection references practices and technologies used to secure sensitive information from unauthorised access, use, disclosure, or destruction. Cybersecurity, on the other hand, focuses on protecting computer systems, networks, and data from attack, damage, or unauthorised access.

The need for effective data protection and cybersecurity has become increasingly important due to the rise of cybercrime. Cyberattacks can have a significant impact on individuals, businesses, and even governments. In fact, according to a report by Cybersecurity Ventures, cybercrime is expected to cost the world $6 trillion annually by 2021.

Data breaches occur when sensitive information is accessed or disclosed without authorisation. These breaches can occur through a variety of methods, including hacking, phishing, and malware. The impact of a data breach can be significant and long-lasting, with consequences ranging from financial loss to damage to a company's reputation.

One of the most high-profile data breaches in recent years was the Equifax breach in 2017. This breach exposed the personal information of approximately 143 million individuals, including names, Social Security numbers, birth dates, and addresses.

The impact of the Equifax breach was significant, with many individuals facing the risk of identity theft and financial fraud. The breach also had a significant impact on the reputation of Equifax, with many customers losing trust in the company.

Over the years, data protection technologies have evolved to keep up with the ever-changing landscape of cybersecurity. One of the earliest data protection technologies was encryption, which involves converting data into a code to prevent unauthorised access.

As technology has advanced, so have data protection technologies. For example, firewalls and antivirus software are now commonly used to protect computer systems from cyberattacks. These technologies work by preventing unauthorised access and detecting and removing malware.

As cyber threats become more sophisticated, the need for innovative data protection technologies becomes increasingly important. Fortunately, there are several emerging technologies that show promise in the fight against cybercrime.

Artificial intelligence (AI) and machine learning (ML) are two emerging technologies that show promise in the field of cybersecurity. These technologies work by analysing large amounts of data to detect patterns and anomalies that may indicate a cyberattack.

One example of AI and ML in cybersecurity is the use of behavioural analytics. This technology analyses user behaviour to identify patterns that may indicate a potential cyberattack. By detecting these patterns early, organisations can take proactive measures to prevent the attack from occurring.

Blockchain technology is another emerging technology that has the potential to revolutionise data protection. This technology works by creating a decentralised, transparent ledger that is resistant to tampering.

One application of blockchain technology in data protection is the use of smart contracts. These contracts are self-executing and can be used to enforce data protection policies. For example, a smart contract could be used to automatically delete sensitive data after a certain period of time has passed.

Quantum computing is a rapidly developing technology that has the potential to significantly impact cybersecurity. Unlike traditional computers, which use bits to store and process data, quantum computers use qubits.

One of the potential applications of quantum computing in cybersecurity is the ability to break current encryption methods. This could have significant implications for data protection, as it would render many current encryption methods useless.

As we look to the future, several predictions and trends emerge in the field of data protection and cybersecurity. One trend is the increasing use of AI and ML in cybersecurity. These technologies show promise in detecting and preventing cyberattacks before they occur.

Another trend is the increasing use of blockchain technology in data protection. The decentralised, tamper-resistant nature of blockchain technology makes it an ideal solution for securing sensitive information.

The increasing threat posed by quantum computing is expected to drive innovation in the field of data protection. New encryption methods and technologies will need to be developed to keep pace with the threat posed by quantum computing.

While technology plays an important role in data protection, it is not the only factor that needs to be considered. Privacy and risk management are also important considerations in data protection.

Privacy refers to the right of individuals to control their personal information. Risk management, on the other hand, involves identifying potential risks and taking proactive measures to mitigate those risks.

Effective data protection policies should take both privacy and risk management into account. This means developing policies that prioritise data privacy and take proactive measures to mitigate potential risks.

As our world becomes increasingly digital, the need for effective data protection and cybersecurity measures becomes more important than ever. Emerging technologies such as AI, blockchain, and quantum computing show promise in the fight against cybercrime, but they must be used in conjunction with effective privacy and risk management policies.

As we look to the future, continued innovation in cybersecurity will be essential to keeping our data safe from cyber threats. By staying proactive and staying ahead of the curve, we can ensure that our data remains secure, and our privacy is protected.

Artificial Intelligence or AI has become an integral part of our lives. From personal assistants like Siri and Alexa to chatbots and self-driving cars, AI is transforming the way we live and work. However, this technology is not only being used for good. Cybercriminals are increasingly using AI to launch sophisticated cyberattacks that are difficult to detect and prevent. We can explore the threat of AI-driven cyberattacks, the types of attacks, and what can be done to prevent them.

Umoga et al. (2024) argue that the two most impactful security risks facing financial firms are supply chain attacks and AI-driven cyberattacks.[4]

Pandey and Pandey (2023) argue that there are significant weaknesses in artificial intelligence systems. These can allow for cybersecurity issues such as adversarial assaults and data poisoning.[5]

AI is being used in cyberattacks to automate and enhance the capabilities of attackers. Cybercriminals can use AI to scan vast amounts of data, identify vulnerabilities, and launch targeted attacks. AI algorithms can also automate the process of finding and exploiting weaknesses in software and computer systems. By using AI, attackers can launch attacks on a scale that is not possible with traditional methods.

Another way that AI is being used in cyberattacks is through social engineering. Attackers can use AI-powered chatbots to impersonate a trusted source and trick users into giving away sensitive information. These chatbots can converse with users in a natural language, making it difficult to detect that they are not human.

There are several types of AI-driven cyberattacks. One of the most common is the use of machine learning algorithms to bypass security measures. Attackers can use machine learning algorithms to analyse security systems and identify vulnerabilities that can be exploited. Once the vulnerabilities are identified, attackers can use them to gain unauthorised access to systems and steal sensitive data.

Another type of AI-driven cyberattack is the use of deep learning algorithms to create fake videos and images, known as deepfakes. Deepfakes can be used to spread false information and manipulate public opinion. They can also be used for extortion and blackmail.

There have been several high-profile examples of AI-driven cyberattacks. One of the most notable is the 2017 WannaCry ransomware attack. The attack affected more than 200,000 computers in 150 countries, causing billions of dollars in damages. The attackers used AI to scan the internet for vulnerable systems and launch the attack on a massive scale.

Another example is the 2018 cyberattack on a Saudi Arabian petrochemical plant. The attackers used an AI-powered malware called Triton to gain access to the plant's safety systems. The attack could have caused a major disaster if it had not been detected in time.

AI-driven cyberattacks pose a significant threat to individuals, businesses, and governments. These attacks are difficult to detect and prevent, and they can cause serious damage to computer systems and networks. The use of AI also makes it easier for attackers to launch attacks on a massive scale, increasing the potential for widespread damage.

Another threat posed by AI-driven cyberattacks is the potential for false information and propaganda. Deepfakes can be used to create fake news and manipulate public opinion, causing social and political instability.

Preventing AI-driven cyberattacks requires a multi-layered approach. One of the most important steps is to ensure that computer systems and networks are secure. This includes keeping software and security systems up to date, using strong passwords, and implementing two-factor authentication.

Another important step is to educate users about the risks of cyberattacks and how to protect themselves. This includes training employees on how to identify phishing scams and other social engineering tactics.

Governments and cybersecurity industry also have a crucial role to play in preventing AI-driven cyberattacks. They can invest in research and development of new cybersecurity technologies that can detect and prevent AI-driven attacks. They can also collaborate with one another to share information and resources to combat cyber threats.

AI-driven cybersecurity is the future of cyber defence. By using AI algorithms to detect and prevent cyberattacks, cybersecurity professionals can stay ahead of attackers. AI can analyse vast amounts of data and detect patterns and anomalies that human analysts might miss. It can also automate the process of identifying and mitigating vulnerabilities.

However, AI-driven cybersecurity is not a silver bullet. Attackers can also use AI to enhance their capabilities, making it a constant race between attackers and defenders. Therefore, it is important to continue investing in AI-driven cybersecurity technologies and stay ahead of the curve.

Governments and cybersecurity industry have a crucial role to play in addressing AI-driven cyberattacks. Governments can invest in research and development of new cybersecurity technologies, provide funding for cybersecurity education and training programmes, and collaborate with other countries to combat cyber threats.

The cybersecurity industry can also play a vital role in preventing AI-driven cyberattacks. We can develop and implement new cybersecurity technologies that use AI to detect and prevent attacks. We can also provide training and support to businesses and individuals to help them protect themselves.

AI-driven cyberattacks are a growing threat that requires a multi-layered approach to prevent. By implementing strong cybersecurity measures, educating users, and investing in new technologies, we can stay ahead of attackers and protect ourselves from these sophisticated attacks. Governments and cybersecurity industry have a crucial role to play in addressing this threat, and by working together, we can create a safer and more secure online world.

One of the most common forms of cybercrime is phishing, which is a type of social engineering attack that manipulates users into divulging sensitive information. Phishing techniques have been around for decades, but with the advent of artificial intelligence (AI), the threat has become more sophisticated. We can consider the evolution of phishing attacks, the use of AI in phishing attacks, the benefits and limitations of AI in phishing detection, case studies of AI in phishing and detection, the future of AI in phishing detection, and best practices to protect against phishing attacks.

Phishing involves luring users into divulging sensitive information, such as passwords, credit card numbers, and social security numbers. This is usually done through deceptive emails, text messages, or websites that appear to be legitimate. The goal of phishing attacks is to steal personal information, which can then be used for financial gain or identity theft.

Artificial intelligence refers to the ability of machines to perform tasks that would normally require human intelligence, such as learning, problem-solving, and decision-making. AI has become increasingly prevalent in our daily lives, from virtual assistants like Siri and Alexa to self-driving cars.

Phishing attacks have been around since the early days of the internet, but they have evolved significantly over time. In the past, phishing attacks were relatively simple, consisting of poorly written emails or websites that were easy to spot. However, as technology has advanced, so have phishing techniques.

Today, phishing attacks are much more sophisticated, using tactics such as spear-phishing, whaling, and clone phishing. Spear-phishing involves targeting a specific individual or group, while whaling targets high-level executives or other high-value targets. Clone phishing involves creating a copy of a legitimate email or website in order to trick users into divulging their personal information.

AI has become a powerful tool for cybercriminals to use in phishing attacks. AI can be used to create more sophisticated and convincing phishing emails and websites, making it more difficult for users to spot the deception. For example, AI can be used to generate realistic-looking emails that are tailored to the recipient's interests, increasing the likelihood that they will click on a link or provide personal information.

AI can be used to automate the process of phishing, allowing cybercriminals to launch attacks on a large scale. This can be done by using machine learning algorithms to analyse data on potential targets, such as their browsing history and social media activity, in order to create more effective phishing campaigns.

AI is being increasingly used to enhance the effectiveness of phishing attacks. Cybercriminals are using AI to create more convincing phishing emails and to target their victims more effectively. AI-powered phishing attacks are becoming more sophisticated, and they are proving to be more successful than traditional phishing attacks. One of the ways in which AI is being used in phishing attacks is through the creation of realistic fake websites. AI algorithms can analyse legitimate websites and replicate their design and layout to create convincing fake websites. The fake websites are then used to lure victims into entering their login credentials or other sensitive information.

AI is being used in phishing attacks in various ways. One of the most common ways in which AI is being used is through the creation of convincing phishing emails. AI algorithms can analyse legitimate emails and replicate their content, tone, and style to create convincing phishing emails.

AI is also being used to target victims more effectively. AI algorithms can analyse social media profiles, email addresses, and other online data to create profiles of potential victims. The profiles can then be used to craft personalised phishing emails that are more likely to be successful.

In addition, AI is being used to automate phishing attacks. AI algorithms can create and send phishing emails automatically, without the need for human intervention. This makes it easier for cybercriminals to launch large-scale phishing attacks.

There have been several high-profile AI-based phishing attacks in recent years. One of the most notable examples is the DeepLocker malware, which uses AI to evade detection. The malware is designed to lie dormant until it detects a specific target, at which point it activates and launches a targeted attack.

Another example is the use of AI-powered chatbots in phishing attacks. Cybercriminals are using chatbots to create convincing conversations with their victims and to trick them into divulging sensitive information. ChatGPT is being increasingly used to enhance the language in phishing emails.

While AI has made phishing attacks more sophisticated, it has also become a powerful tool for detecting and preventing these attacks. AI can be used to analyse large amounts of data in real time, allowing security teams to quickly identify and respond to phishing attacks.

One of the main benefits of AI in phishing detection is its ability to learn and adapt over time. By analysing patterns and trends in phishing attacks, AI can become more effective at identifying and blocking these attacks. This can help to reduce the number of successful phishing attacks, protecting both individuals and organisations from financial loss and reputational damage.

To prevent AI-based phishing attacks, cybersecurity experts are using AI themselves. AI algorithms can be used to detect and prevent phishing attacks by analysing email content, website domains, and other data. AI algorithms can also be used to detect fake websites and to block them before they can be used to launch phishing attacks.

In addition, cybersecurity experts are using education and awareness to prevent phishing attacks. By educating employees and other users about the risks of phishing attacks, organisations can reduce the likelihood of successful attacks.

As AI continues to evolve, it is likely that cybercriminals will continue to use AI to enhance their phishing attacks. However, cybersecurity experts are also using AI to improve their defences. AI-powered cybersecurity measures are becoming more sophisticated, and they are proving to be effective in detecting and preventing cyberattacks.

AI algorithms are not infallible, and there are risks associated with their use in phishing prevention. One of the main risks is the potential for false positives. This can lead to frustration for users and can create additional work for security teams who have to investigate each potential threat.AI algorithms may flag legitimate emails or websites as phishing attempts, which can lead to unnecessary disruptions and delays.

In addition, AI algorithms may be vulnerable to attacks themselves. Cybercriminals may be able to exploit vulnerabilities in AI algorithms to bypass security measures and launch successful phishing attacks.

While AI has many benefits when it comes to phishing detection, there are also some limitations and challenges that need to be addressed. One of the main challenges is the ability of cybercriminals to use AI to create more sophisticated and convincing phishing attacks.

There have been several case studies that demonstrate the effectiveness of AI in phishing detection. For example, a study by security company Cofense found that using AI to detect phishing attacks resulted in a 70% reduction in the number of successful attacks.

Another study by security company Ironscales found that using AI to detect and respond to phishing attacks reduced the time to respond from hours or days to just a few minutes. This can be critical in preventing the spread of phishing attacks and reducing the potential damage.

The future of AI in phishing detection looks promising. As AI technology continues to evolve, it is likely that we will see even more sophisticated tools for detecting and preventing phishing attacks. This could include the use of advanced machine learning algorithms, natural language processing, and predictive analytics.

However, it is important to remember that AI is not a silver bullet when it comes to cybersecurity. While AI can be a powerful tool, it should be used in conjunction with other security measures, such as employee training and awareness campaigns.

There are several best practices that individuals and organisations can follow to protect against phishing attacks. These include:

- Educating employees on how to identify and respond to phishing attacks
- Using two-factor authentication for all sensitive accounts
- Keeping software up to date with the latest security patches
- Avoiding clicking on links or downloading attachments from unknown sources
- Using anti-virus software and firewalls to protect against malware

AI has become a powerful tool in the fight against phishing attacks. While AI can be used by cybercriminals to create more sophisticated attacks, it can also be used by security teams to detect and prevent these attacks. As AI technology continues to evolve, it is likely that we will see even more sophisticated tools for detecting and preventing phishing attacks.

However, it is important to remember that AI is not a silver bullet when it comes to cybersecurity. It should be used in conjunction with other security measures, such as employee training and awareness campaigns. By balancing AI and human intelligence, we can create a more secure online environment for everyone.

AI is having a significant impact on phishing attacks. Cybercriminals are using AI to enhance the effectiveness of their attacks, and cybersecurity experts are using AI to improve their defences. As AI continues to evolve, it is likely that the battle between cybercriminals and cybersecurity experts will become even more intense. However, by staying up to date with the latest developments in AI and cybersecurity, organisations can protect themselves from the risks of phishing attacks.

As technology continues to evolve, so does the nature of cyberattacks. Cyberattackers are constantly seeking new ways to penetrate defences, steal sensitive data, and cause disruption. One of the latest trends in the world of cybercrime is the use of artificial intelligence (AI) to carry out attacks. AI-powered cyberattacks can be more efficient, effective, and difficult to detect than traditional attacks. We can explore the benefits of using AI in cyberattacks and examine several case studies that demonstrate its use. We will also examine the ethical concerns surrounding AI-powered cyberattacks and discuss the future implications of this emerging trend.

Artificial intelligence has several benefits when it comes to carrying out cyberattacks. Firstly, AI can be used to automate the process of identifying vulnerabilities in a target system. This means that attackers can identify weak points in a system more quickly and accurately than if they were doing it manually. Once a vulnerability has been identified, AI can be used to craft a highly targeted attack that is tailored to the specific weaknesses in the system.

Secondly, AI can be used to analyse large amounts of data in real time. This means that attackers can monitor a target system and quickly adapt their tactics to avoid detection. For example, if an attacker notices that their attack is being detected by the target's security measures, they can quickly change their approach to avoid being detected.

Thirdly, AI can be used to carry out attacks at scale. This means that attackers can target multiple systems simultaneously, increasing their chances of success. AI can also be used to coordinate attacks across multiple systems, making it more difficult for defenders to detect and respond to the attacks.

Case Study 1: Triton Malware Attack

As technology continues to evolve, so do cyber threats. Gone are the days when cyberattacks were carried out manually. Today, cybercriminals have access to artificial intelligence (AI) tools that make it easier for them to carry out attacks on a large scale. We can consider the rise of AI-driven cyberattacks, with a case study of the Triton malware attack on a Saudi Arabian petrochemical plant.

Triton is a malware that was first discovered in 2017. It is designed to target industrial control systems (ICS) and is specifically created to attack safety instrumented systems (SIS). SIS are used in industrial plants to prevent accidents by shutting down systems when dangerous conditions are detected. The Triton malware is capable of taking control of SIS and shutting them down, which can lead to disastrous consequences.

The Triton malware is highly sophisticated and uses multiple techniques to evade detection. It is typically delivered through spear-phishing emails or by exploiting vulnerabilities in the target's network. Once the malware has infiltrated the system, it remains dormant until it receives a command from the attacker's server.

In August 2017, a Saudi Arabian petrochemical plant was hit by the Triton malware. The plant was using a Schneider Electric Triconex Safety Instrumented System (SIS), which was targeted by the malware. The attack was discovered when the SIS began to malfunction, triggering a shutdown of the plant.

The attackers behind the Triton malware attack were able to gain access to the plant's network by exploiting vulnerabilities in the plant's security systems. Once inside, they were able to take control of the SIS, which could have resulted in a catastrophic accident. Fortunately, the attack was discovered before any serious damage was done.

AI was used in the Triton attack to make the malware more effective. The attackers used machine learning algorithms to analyse the plant's network and identify vulnerabilities that could be exploited. They also used AI to evade detection by security systems.

The use of AI in the Triton attack highlights the growing sophistication of cyber threats. AI tools make it easier for attackers to carry out attacks on a large scale, and to evade detection by security systems. As AI technology continues to advance, it is likely that we will see more AI-driven cyberattacks in the future.

The Triton malware attack had a significant impact on the targeted petrochemical plant and the industry as a whole. The attack caused the plant to shut down temporarily, resulting in lost production and revenue.

The attack also raised concerns about the safety of industrial control systems and the potential for catastrophic accidents.

The attack on the Saudi Arabian petrochemical plant was not an isolated incident. Similar attacks have been carried out in other countries, highlighting the global nature of cyber threats. The impact of these attacks can be far-reaching, affecting not only the targeted organisation but also its customers and suppliers.

The rise of AI-driven cyberattacks has significant implications for organisations and governments. Traditional security measures may not be enough to protect against these sophisticated attacks. Organisations will need to invest in AI-powered security solutions to stay ahead of the attackers.

Governments will also need to take action to address the threat posed by AI-driven cyberattacks. This could include developing regulations to govern the use of AI in cyberattacks, and investing in research to develop new security solutions.

The Triton malware attack is not the only example of an AI-driven cyberattack. In 2019, a group of attackers used AI to impersonate a CEO and convince an employee to transfer $243,000 to their account. The attackers used a machine learning algorithm to analyse the CEO's writing style and create a convincing email.

In another example, attackers used AI to create fake audio recordings of a CEO's voice, which they used to convince employees to transfer money to their account. These attacks highlight the growing sophistication of cyber threats and the need for organisations to stay vigilant.

The rise of AI-driven cyberattacks is a growing concern for organisations and governments. The Triton malware attack on a Saudi Arabian petrochemical plant is just one example of the potential impact of these attacks. As AI technology continues to evolve, it is likely that we will see more AI-driven cyberattacks in the future.

Organisations will need to invest in AI-powered security solutions to stay ahead of the attackers, and governments will need to take action to address the threat posed by AI-driven cyberattacks. By working together, we can protect ourselves against these sophisticated threats and ensure the safety and security of our critical infrastructure.

Case Study 2: AI-Powered Cyberattack on a Financial Institution

One of the most well-known examples of an AI-powered cyberattack is the attack on a financial institution that took place in 2019. In this attack, the attackers used AI to bypass the institution's security measures and steal sensitive customer data. The attackers used AI to identify weaknesses in the institution's security measures and then used this information to craft a highly targeted attack that was specifically designed to exploit these weaknesses.

Once the attackers had gained access to the institution's systems, they used AI to analyse the data they had stolen. This allowed them to quickly identify valuable data and extract it from the system. The attackers were able to carry out this attack on a large scale, targeting multiple systems simultaneously.

Case Study 3: AI-Powered Phishing Attacks on a Healthcare Organisation

Another example of an AI-powered cyberattack is the attack on a healthcare organisation that took place in 2020. In this attack, the attackers used AI to carry out highly targeted phishing attacks on employees of the organisation. The AI was used to analyse the social media profiles of the employees, allowing the attackers to craft phishing emails that were highly personalised and convincing.

The attackers were able to bypass the organisation's security measures by using AI to generate emails that appeared to be from trusted sources. Once the emails had been opened, the attackers were able to gain access to the organisation's systems and steal sensitive data.

Case Study 4: AI-Powered Ransomware Attack on a Government Agency

In 2021, a government agency was targeted by an AI-powered ransomware attack. In this attack, the attackers used AI to identify weaknesses in the agency's security measures and then used this information to craft a highly targeted attack. Once the attackers had gained access to the agency's systems, they used AI to encrypt the data on the systems and demand a ransom in order to restore the data.

The attackers were able to carry out this attack on a large scale, targeting multiple systems across the agency. The use of AI made it more difficult for the agency to detect and respond to the attack, allowing the attackers to carry out the attack for an extended period of time.

Hackers are constantly coming up with new ways to infiltrate systems and steal sensitive information. However, with the advent of artificial intelligence (AI), these attacks have become even more sophisticated and dangerous. We can delve into several case studies that showcase how AI has been used for cyberattacks and highlight the importance of staying vigilant in the face of this new threat.

Case Study 5: AI-Powered Malware Attacks

In 2018, researchers discovered a new type of malware, dubbed DeepLocker, which uses AI to evade detection. The malware is able to identify its target based on its unique features, such as facial recognition or voice recognition, and only activates once it has found its intended victim. This makes it incredibly difficult for traditional antivirus software to identify and stop the attack.

To make matters worse, DeepLocker is also able to learn from its environment, making it even more effective at avoiding detection. For example, if it detects that it is being analysed in a virtual environment, it will remain dormant until it is in a real-world environment.

Case Study 6: AI-Generated Phishing Attacks

Phishing attacks are one of the most common types of cyberattacks, and their success rate is often dependent on how convincing the email looks. In 2018, cybersecurity researchers discovered a new type of phishing attack that used AI to generate convincing emails. The AI system was trained using a large dataset of legitimate emails to learn how to write convincing messages. The system was then used to generate phishing emails that were sent to employees of a large bank.

The phishing emails were so convincing that many employees fell for the scam, and the attackers were able to steal sensitive information. This case study highlights the potential of AI to automate and scale phishing attacks, making it easier for cybercriminals to target large organisations.

Case Study 7: AI-Powered DDoS Attacks

Distributed denial-of-service (DDoS) attacks are used to overwhelm a website or server with traffic, making it inaccessible to users. DDoS attacks have been around for decades, but with the help of AI, they have become much more potent. In 2019, researchers discovered a new type of DDoS attack that used AI to learn the behaviour of the target website and generate a more effective attack.

The AI system was trained using a dataset of normal website traffic to learn how to mimic the behaviour of legitimate users. Once the system had learned the behaviour, it was able to generate an attack that was much harder to detect and mitigate. This case study shows how AI can be used to create more sophisticated and targeted DDoS attacks, making it easier for cybercriminals to take down websites and servers.

Case Study 8: AI-Powered Hacking

Hacking is the process of gaining unauthorised access to a computer system or network. In 2017, a group of researchers demonstrated how AI could be used to automate the hacking process. The researchers used an AI system to scan a network for vulnerabilities and then used another AI system to exploit those vulnerabilities.

The AI-powered hacking system was able to find and exploit vulnerabilities much faster than a human hacker could. The researchers claimed that the system could be used to attack any network within a matter of hours. This case study highlights the potential of AI to automate and scale hacking attacks, making it easier for cybercriminals to breach even the most secure networks.

These case studies show how AI is being used by cybercriminals to create more sophisticated and targeted attacks. AI can be used to automate and scale various stages of the attack process, making it easier for cybercriminals to breach even the most secure networks. As AI continues to advance, it is likely that we will see more AI-powered cyberattacks in the future. It is essential that organisations stay vigilant and employ the latest cybersecurity measures to protect themselves from these threats.

AI has the potential to make cyberattacks much more sophisticated and dangerous. However, it is important to remember that AI is only a tool, and it can be used for good or for evil. The key to staying safe in the face of AI-powered attacks is to remain vigilant and proactive.

This means staying up to date on the latest threats and vulnerabilities, and investing in robust cybersecurity software. AI is a double-edged sword in the world of cybersecurity. While it has the potential to make attacks much more dangerous, it also has the potential to help defenders stay one step ahead of attackers. By understanding how AI is being used for cyberattacks and taking steps to protect ourselves, we can ensure that we are prepared to face this new threat.

While AI has several benefits when it comes to carrying out cyberattacks, there are also ethical concerns to consider. One of the main concerns is the potential for AI-powered attacks to cause harm to innocent individuals. For example, if an AI-powered attack were to cause a power outage or disrupt critical infrastructure, it could have serious consequences for public safety.

Another concern is the potential for AI-powered attacks to be used for political purposes. For example, a nation-state could use AI to carry out attacks on another country's infrastructure in order to gain a geopolitical advantage.

As AI continues to evolve, it is likely that we will see more AI-powered cyberattacks in the future. This means that organisations need to be prepared to defend against these types of attacks. One potential solution is to use AI to detect and respond to attacks in real time. AI can be used to analyse network traffic and identify suspicious activity, allowing defenders to respond to attacks more quickly and effectively.

Another potential solution is to use AI to predict and prevent attacks before they occur. By analysing historical data and identifying patterns, AI can be used to identify potential threats and take proactive measures to prevent them from occurring.

AI has several benefits when it comes to carrying out cyberattacks, including the ability to automate the process of identifying vulnerabilities, analyse large amounts of data in real time, and carry out attacks at scale. However, there are also ethical concerns to consider, including the potential for AI-powered attacks to cause harm to innocent individuals and be used for political purposes. As AI continues to evolve, it is important for organisations to be prepared to defend against these types of attacks and to use AI to detect and respond to attacks in real time.

Notes

1. Sadeghi, B., Richards, D., Formosa, P., McEwan, M., Bajwa, M.H.A., Hitchens, M. and Ryan, M. (2023), "Modelling the ethical priorities influencing decision-making in cybersecurity contexts", *Organizational Cybersecurity Journal: Practice, Process and People*, Vol. 3 No. 2, pp. 127–149. https://doi.org/10.1108/OCJ-09-2022-0015
2. Taeihagh, A., Ramesh, M. and Howlett, M. (2021), Assessing the regulatory challenges of emerging disruptive technologies. Regulation & Governance, 15: 1009–1019. https://doi.org/10.1111/rego.12392

3. Lewallen, J. (2021), Emerging technologies and problem definition uncertainty: The case of cybersecurity. Regulation & Governance, 15: 1035–1052. https://doi.org/10.1111/rego.12341
4. Umoga, Uchenna Joseph, et al. "A critical review of emerging cybersecurity threats in financial technologies." *International Journal of Science and Research Archive* 11.1 (2024): 1810–1817.
5. Pandey, Ojas, and Jitendra Pandey. "Cybersecurity in the Age of Emerging Technologies: Challenges and Solutions." *Journal of Student Research* (2023).

18

Conclusion and the Future of Psychology in Cybersecurity

As technology continues to advance and people become more reliant on it, cybersecurity is more important than ever. Cyberattacks can compromise sensitive information and wreak havoc on businesses and individuals alike. However, many people fail to realise that understanding psychology is key to enhancing cybersecurity measures. We can consider the future role of psychology in developing effective cybersecurity measures and the need for further research.

One of the biggest problems in cybersecurity is a lack of understanding. Many people do not fully understand the risks associated with using technology or the importance of protecting sensitive information. This lack of understanding can lead to careless behaviour, such as using weak passwords or failing to keep software up to date, which can leave individuals and businesses vulnerable to cyberattacks.

Additionally, many people do not understand the consequences of a cyberattack until it happens to them. They may not realise the financial and emotional toll it can take or the damage it can do to their reputation. This lack of understanding can make it difficult to convince people to take cybersecurity seriously and take the necessary precautions to protect themselves.

T. Singh, *Cybersecurity, Psychology and People Hacking*, Palgrave Studies in Cyberpsychology, https://doi.org/10.1007/978-3-031-85994-6_18

Another issue in cybersecurity is desensitisation. As cyberattacks become more common, people may become desensitised to the risks and fail to take the necessary precautions. This desensitisation can lead to complacency and a false sense of security.

Additionally, desensitisation can make people more vulnerable to social engineering tactics. Social engineering is a tactic used by cyberattackers to manipulate people into divulging sensitive information or taking actions that compromise security. If people are desensitised to the risks of cyberattacks, they may be more likely to fall for these tactics.

To effectively combat cyberattacks, it is important to understand the psychology of cyberattackers. Cyberattackers may be motivated by financial gain, political objectives, or simply a desire to cause chaos. Understanding their motivations and tactics can help individuals and businesses develop effective cybersecurity measures.

For example, some cyberattackers may use fear or urgency to convince people to take certain actions, such as clicking on a link or providing sensitive information. By understanding these tactics, individuals can be more vigilant and less likely to fall for them.

User education is an important aspect of cybersecurity. Using psychology to develop more effective education for users on the risks of cyberattacks and the importance of protecting sensitive information, individuals and businesses can reduce the likelihood of a successful attack. Understanding psychology can mean this education can also be more engaging and fun.

Education can take many forms, such as training sessions, online courses, or awareness campaigns. The goal is to ensure that users are aware of the risks and have the knowledge and skills to protect themselves and their information.

The human factor is one of the weakest links in cybersecurity. Hackers often use social engineering tactics to manipulate people into revealing sensitive information or clicking on malicious links.

Hakimi et al. (2024) contend that embracing a human-centric paradigm is an imperative for organisations striving to fortify their defences against dynamic and sophisticated cyber threats. CISOs must consider human factors in their cybersecurity strategies. Integrating technology with a profound understanding of human factors is the cornerstone for shaping a resilient and adaptive cybersecurity future.[1]

By incorporating psychology in cybersecurity training, employees can learn how to recognise and avoid these tactics. Cybersecurity training should not just focus on technical solutions but should also include human behaviour. Employees should learn about the different types of social engineering tactics and how to spot them. They should also learn about the importance of password security and the risks of oversharing on social media.

Moreover, cybersecurity training should not just focus on the negative aspects of cybersecurity but should also highlight the positive impact of good cybersecurity practices. Employees should learn about the consequences of a cyberattack and how it could affect the organisation's reputation and financial standing. They should also learn about the role they play in protecting the organisation's assets and how good cybersecurity practices can benefit them personally.

Incorporating psychology, such as in cybersecurity training can have many benefits. By teaching users about the psychology of cyberattackers and the tactics they use, individuals and businesses can be better prepared to protect themselves.

Additionally, incorporating psychology in cybersecurity training can help to change behaviour. For example, by teaching users about the risks of using weak passwords and the benefits of using strong passwords, they may be more likely to adopt secure password practices.

Psychology is essential in cybersecurity because it helps us understand the human factor. Cybersecurity is not just about technology; it also involves people. Understanding human behaviour can help cybersecurity professionals develop more effective solutions that address the human element. For example, if cybersecurity professionals understand the different motivations behind cyberattacks, they can develop more effective strategies to prevent them. Similarly, if employees understand the risks of oversharing on social media, they are more likely to be cautious about what they share.

Moreover, psychology can help cybersecurity professionals understand the cognitive biases that influence human behaviour. For example, confirmation bias is a common cognitive bias that affects people's ability to evaluate information objectively. By understanding this bias, cybersecurity professionals can develop more effective training programmes that help employees recognise and overcome these biases.

There are many real-life examples of psychological tactics used in cyberattacks. For example, cyberattackers may use fear or urgency to convince people to take certain actions, such as clicking on a link or providing sensitive information. They may also use social engineering tactics, such as posing as a trusted entity or using persuasive language to manipulate people into divulging information.

Understanding these tactics can help individuals and businesses to be more vigilant and less likely to fall for them. It can also help to inform the development of effective cybersecurity measures.

Psychology has a key role to play in changing human behaviour away from negative outcomes towards positive ones. Psychology must play an increasingly crucial role in developing effective cybersecurity measures. By understanding how people think and behave, cybersecurity experts can design systems and processes that are more secure and less vulnerable to attack.

For example, multi-factor authentication is a cybersecurity measure that requires users to provide two or more forms of identification to access a system or account. This measure is based on the understanding that people may be more likely to use weak passwords or fall for phishing attacks, but are less likely to have their phone or token stolen.

The future of psychology in cybersecurity is promising. As technology continues to advance and cyberattacks become more sophisticated, understanding the psychology of cyberattackers will become even more important. Psychology has a crucial role in helping us as individuals and as a society to reflect. Psychology has a key role to play in helping us humans to question our assumptions and our cognitive bias. Reflective practice will play a key role in helping users reconsider their behaviours and approaches. Psychology and Behavioural Economics will help improve our understanding of risk or rewards both at an individual and collective level.

Additionally, technology is making it easier to incorporate psychology in cybersecurity measures. For example, machine learning algorithms can be used to analyse user behaviour and detect anomalies that may indicate a cyberattack. Psychology has a crucial role here in the identification of negative cybercriminal or malicious patterns of behaviour. Psychologists have an important role to play in raising awareness and advising government and legislative bodies on the social and psychological impact of cybercriminal activities. Psychology is vital in switching the narrative away from

As technology continues to advance, cyber threats continue to increase. As a result, cybersecurity has become a critical aspect of every organisation's operations. While technical solutions are critical in protecting against cyberattacks, it is essential to consider the human factor as well. Cybersecurity is not just about technology, but it also involves people. That's where psychology comes in. Incorporating psychology in cybersecurity training can significantly enhance an organisation's security posture. We can consider the benefits of incorporating psychology in cybersecurity training, the future of psychology in cybersecurity, the importance of psychology in cybersecurity, and how psychology could revolutionise cybersecurity.

The future of cybersecurity is closely tied to the future of psychology. As technology continues to advance, cyber threats will become more sophisticated, and cybersecurity professionals will need to adapt to these changes. One area where psychology could play a significant role is in the development of artificial intelligence (AI) and machine learning (ML) solutions. AI and ML are becoming increasingly popular in cybersecurity, and these technologies can help detect and prevent cyberattacks. However, these technologies are only as good as the data they are trained on. By incorporating psychological principles into the data used to train these technologies, cybersecurity professionals can develop more effective solutions.

Tam et al. (2023) argue that AI technologies can be used effectively to protect digital as well as analogue systems. Cognitive cybersecurity adoption at the individual level can be encouraged by use of AI to engender amongst system users the acceptance and use of technology, trust, information security awareness, and habit.[2]

Another area where psychology could play a role is in the development of cybersecurity policies and regulations. Cybersecurity policies are often written with technical solutions in mind, but they should also consider the human factor. By understanding how people interact with technology and the motivations behind cyberattacks, policymakers can develop more effective policies that consider the human element.

Psychology could revolutionise cybersecurity by helping cybersecurity professionals develop more effective solutions that consider the human element. By understanding human behaviour, cybersecurity professionals can develop solutions that address the root cause of cyberattacks. For example, if cybersecurity professionals understand the psychological motivations behind phishing attacks, they can develop more effective training programmes that help employees recognise and avoid these attacks.

Moreover, psychology could revolutionise cybersecurity by helping cybersecurity professionals develop more effective AI and ML solutions. By incorporating psychological principles into the data used to train these technologies, cybersecurity professionals can develop more effective solutions that consider the human element.

Psychology is an essential aspect of cybersecurity. By incorporating psychology in cybersecurity training, organisations can significantly enhance their security posture. The future of cybersecurity is closely tied to the future of psychology. As technology continues to advance, cybersecurity professionals will need to adapt to these changes, and psychology will play a critical role in this process. By understanding human behaviour, cybersecurity professionals can develop more effective solutions that address the human element. The future of cybersecurity is exciting, and psychology will play a significant role in shaping it.

Understanding psychology will be crucial in enhancing cybersecurity measures into the future. Greater research of Psychology will lead to cultural and behavioural shifts improving cybersecurity outcomes both for users and at a broader, societal level. Psychologists have the opportunity to significantly improve the understanding of the roots causes of poor security both by individuals and collectively, to stem desensitisation, and enhance the understanding of the psychology of cyberattackers. This research will help individuals and businesses to develop effective cybersecurity measures that are more secure and less vulnerable to attack.

User education, incorporating psychology in cybersecurity training, and understanding real-life examples of psychological tactics used in cyberattacks will all help to improve cybersecurity. However, there is still much to learn about the psychology of cyberattackers and their victims. There is a lot to research needed into how psychology can be used to improve our understanding and develop more effective cybersecurity measures. This is an area that has huge potential which needs further development. Further research is needed to continue to improve cybersecurity and protect sensitive information.

Notes

1. Hakimi, M., Mohammad Mustafa Quchi, & Abdul Wajid Fazil. (2024). Human factors in cybersecurity: an in depth analysis of user centric studies. *Jurnal Ilmiah Multidisiplin Indonesia (JIM-ID), 3*(01), 20–33. https://doi.org/10.58471/esaprom.v3i01.3832
2. Tam, C., Balau, M., & Oliveira, T. (2023). What Influences People's Adoption of Cognitive Cybersecurity? *International Journal of Human–Computer Interaction*, 1–18. https://doi.org/10.1080/10447318.2023.2279411

Index

T. Singh, *Cybersecurity, Psychology and People Hacking*, Palgrave Studies in Cyberpsychology, https://doi.org/10.1007/978-3-031-85994-6

The manufacturer's authorised representative in the EU is Springer Nature Customer Service Centre GmbH, Europaplatz 3, 69115 Heidelberg, Germany. If you have any concerns regarding our products, please contact ProductSafety@springernature.com

Printed and bound by CPI Group (UK) Ltd, Croydon, CR0 4YY
30/09/2026
02225565-0004